CGP — the only logical choice...

The best way to get ready for the OCR GCSE Computer Science exams is lots (and lots) of practice. That's where this brilliant CGP book comes in...

It's packed with hundreds of realistic exam-style questions, covering everything from basic definitions to the dreaded 8-mark extended answers — plus a good serving of questions to test your practical programming skills.

And with step-by-step answers included at the back of the book, you'll have compressed all the exam data into your memory in no time.

CGP — still the best! ☺

Our sole aim here at CGP is to produce the highest quality books — carefully written, immaculately presented and dangerously close to being funny.

Then we work our socks off to get them out to you — at the cheapest possible prices.

Contents

✓ Use the tick boxes to check off the topics you've completed.

Component 01 — Computer Systems

Section One — Components of a Computer System

Section Two — Data Representation

Section Three — Networks

Section Four — Issues

Component 02 — Computational Thinking, Algorithms and Programming

Section Five — Algorithms

Section Six — Programming

Section Seven — Design, Testing and IDEs

Published by CGP

Based on the classic CGP style created by Richard Parsons.

Editors: Liam Dyer, Sammy El-Bahrawy, Rob Harrison, Simon Little and Michael Weynberg.

Contributor: Colin Harber-Stuart

With thanks to Shaun Harrogate, Neil Hastings and Richard Campbell for the proofreading.

ISBN: 978 1 78908 557 0

Microsoft® and Windows® are either registered trademarks or trademarks of Microsoft Corporation in the United States and/or other countries.

Android is a trademark of Google LLC.

Exam Reference Language OCR April 2020. OCR maintains the current version of the Exam Reference Language and specification on the OCR website. You should always check for the latest version and any updates. (https://www.ocr.org.uk/qualifications/gcse/computer-science-j277-from-2020/)

Printed by Elanders Ltd, Newcastle upon Tyne
Clipart from Corel®

How to Use This Book

- Hold the book <u>upright</u>, approximately <u>50 cm</u> from your face, ensuring that the text looks like <u>this</u>, not ̅s̅i̅ɥ̅ʇ̅. Alternatively, place the book on a <u>horizontal</u> surface (e.g. a table or desk) and sit adjacent to the book, at a distance which doesn't make the text too small to read.
- In case of emergency, press the two halves of the book together <u>firmly</u> in order to close.
- Before attempting to use this book, familiarise yourself with the following <u>safety information</u>:

The questions are arranged into topics, so you can get exam practice on exactly the bit of your course that you want.

Some topics have warm-up questions to help you get started on the very basics of the topic.

Program Flow

Warm-Up

Put each of these statements into the correct box below.

IF-THEN-ELSE   SWITCH   DO UNTIL   IF-ELSEIF   WHILE

Selection Statements   Iteration Statements

Any code is written in OCR Exam Reference Language (unless the question specifies that it's pseudocode)

1   Jasminda has written the following program to convert minutes into hours and minutes.

```
minutes = input("Enter a number of minutes.")
hours = minutes DIV 60
mins = minutes MOD 60
print(str(hours) + " hours and " + str(mins) + " minutes")
```

a) Which programming construct has been used in this program? Tick the correct box.

Sequence ☐   Selection ☐   Iteration ☐

b) What would the program print if the input was 150?

....

[1]

[Total 2 marks]

You're told how many marks each question part is worth, and then the total for the whole question.

The lines/space below each question will give you enough space to write your full answer.

2   Salik needs a program that will ask users to create a password and then check if the password contains at least six characters. If it contains fewer than six characters the user must try again, otherwise the user is informed that their password is valid.

Write an appropriate program for Salik.

You may want to consider using a DO UNTIL loop in your program.

You have a choice how you present your answer for some questions, e.g. you could write pseudocode, program code or draw a flowchart here.

These contain handy tips to help you with specific questions.

Exam Practice Tips give you hints to help with answering exam questions on certain topics.

Exam Practice Tip

When it comes to writing programs and algorithms in the exam it's important that you remember to lay them out correctly — this means using indentation and finishing statements, e.g. with endif or endswitch. Another key thing to remember is to use == when you mean "is equal to" and = as the assignment operator — otherwise you'll lose marks.

Section Six — Programming   ☹☐   ☺☐   ☺☐

Tick one of these boxes depending on how confident you feel with the questions in each topic. This should help show you where you need to focus your revision.

Exam Tips

Exam Stuff

1) You have to do <u>two exams</u> for your OCR GCSE in Computer Science — Papers 1 and 2.

2) <u>Paper 1</u> focuses on computer systems, data, networks and the impact of digital technology.
<u>Paper 2</u> focuses on algorithms, programming, logic, design and testing. It has two sections:
   - <u>Section A</u> (50 marks) tests your <u>knowledge, understanding and analytical skills</u>. You can give your answers in <u>any suitable format</u> — this might include things like pseudocode or flowcharts.
   - <u>Section B</u> (30 marks) tests your <u>practical programming skills</u>, such as <u>writing</u>, <u>designing</u>, <u>testing</u> and <u>refining</u> programs. Some questions will <u>specify</u> that you should answer in a <u>particular</u> format.

3) Both exams are <u>1½ hours long</u>, and worth <u>80 marks</u>. That means you should aim for a <u>mark per minute</u> and you'll have time to check back through your answers at the end.

4) You are <u>not allowed</u> to use a calculator for either exam.

There are a Few Golden Rules...

Obeying these Golden Rules is no use if you haven't learnt the stuff in the first place. Make sure you revise well and do <u>as many</u> practice questions as you can.

1) **Always, always, always make sure you <u>read the question properly</u>.**
E.g. if you're asked to convert your answer to binary, <u>don't</u> give it in denary.

2) **Look at the <u>number of marks</u> a question is worth.**
The number of marks gives you a pretty good clue of <u>how much</u> to write. There's no point writing an essay for a question that's only worth one mark — it's just a waste of your time.

3) **Write your answers as <u>clearly</u> as you can.**
If the examiner can't read your answer you won't get any marks, even if it's right.

4) **Use the <u>correct terminology</u>.**
It's no good using <u>computery words</u> if you don't know what they mean.

5) **Pay attention to the <u>time</u>.**
If you're totally, hopelessly stuck on a question, just <u>leave it</u> and <u>move on</u> to the next one. You can always <u>go back to it</u> at the end if you've got enough time.

... and some extra tips for Certain Question Types

1) **Extended response questions (Paper 1 only)**
This type of question is worth <u>8 marks</u> — to gain <u>top marks</u> you'll need to show a <u>deep understanding</u> of the topic and give <u>accurate</u> and <u>detailed evidence</u> to back up your points.

2) **Practical programming questions (Paper 2, Section B only)**
You'll need to <u>write</u> or <u>refine</u> a program using <u>precise</u> programming commands, using either the OCR Exam Reference Language or a high-level programming language you've learned.

You Need to Understand the Command Words

<u>Command words</u> are the words in a question that tell you <u>what to do</u>.
If you don't know what they mean, you might not be able to answer the questions properly.

State / Identify — You need to give a <u>short answer</u> (usually just a phrase or number) or <u>select an item</u> from a list of possible answers — no explanation is required.

Define — You need to give the <u>precise meaning</u> of a word, phrase or object.

Describe / Explain — You need to give a <u>detailed account</u> of a process or concept. For 'explain' questions you also need to give <u>reasons</u> or <u>causes</u>.

Discuss / Evaluate — You have to give a <u>balanced argument</u> covering a range of <u>opinions</u> and <u>arguments</u>, backing up each of your points with <u>evidence</u>.

Computer Systems

Warm-Up   Circle the items that are components of a computer system.

RAM   Graphics Card   Motherboard   A Dead Mouse

Hard Disk Drive   REM   Optical Drive   ROOM   Cooling Fan   The Internet   Heat Sink

---

1   Computer systems consist of hardware and software that work together.

a) Define what is meant by hardware. Give **one** example.

Definition: ....

Example: ....

[2]

b) Define what is meant by software. Give **one** example.

Definition: ....

Example: ....

[2]

[Total 4 marks]

---

2   A microwave contains an embedded system which controls its cooking modes.

a) What is an embedded system?

....

[1]

b) Give **two** other examples of devices that may contain an embedded system.

1 ....

2 ....

[2]

c) Explain **two** benefits of using an embedded system in a microwave instead of a general purpose computer.

1 ....

....

2 ....

....

[4]

[Total 7 marks]

The CPU

Write the names of the parts of the CPU in the correct places.

Central Processing Unit

Control Unit

Other Registers

ALU

Input Device

Output Device

Memory

Program Counter (PC)

Memory Address Register (MAR)

Accumulator

Memory Data Register (MDR)

1 Tick **one** box for each statement to show whether it is true or false.

a) CPU stands for Computer Processing Unit. **True** ☐ **False** ☐ *[1]*

b) The CPU processes all of the data and instructions that make a computer system work. **True** ☐ **False** ☐ *[1]*

c) The CPU carries out the fetch-execute cycle. **True** ☐ **False** ☐ *[1]*

d) The clock speed, number of processor cores and cache size all affect CPU performance. **True** ☐ **False** ☐ *[1]*

[Total 4 marks]

2 The control unit, arithmetic logic unit and cache memory are all parts of the CPU.

a) State **two** functions of the Control Unit.

1 ....

2 ....

[2]

b) Describe the function of the Arithmetic Logic Unit (ALU).

....

....

[2]

c) Explain how cache memory is used by the CPU.

....

....

....

[3]

[Total 7 marks]

Section One — Components of a Computer System

3 A tech firm has started producing their own CPUs.
They are currently testing the registers in some prototype CPUs.

a) Explain the purpose of CPU registers.

....

....

[2]

b) Outline the function of each of the following CPU registers:

Accumulator ....

MAR ....

MDR ....

[3]

c) A fault is identified in the prototype CPUs where the program counter is not
incrementing with each cycle. Explain what will happen in the CPU in this case.

....

....

[2]

[Total 7 marks]

4 CPUs process data according to the fetch-execute cycle.

Describe what happens during each stage of the fetch-execute cycle.

....

....

....

....

....

....

....

....

[Total 6 marks]

Exam Practice Tip

Whenever you're asked about the CPU it may help to visualise a diagram like the one on page 5. Make sure you know
what each acronym (e.g. ALU, MAR, MDR, PC) stands for, as this will give you a clue about what each bit does.

Memory

1 Describe the difference between volatile and non-volatile memory.

....

....

[Total 2 marks]

2 Nigel runs a piece of software to analyse the performance of his computer.
It recommends that he should install more RAM in his computer.

a) Explain the purpose of RAM in a computer system.

....

....

[2]

b) Give **two** reasons why Nigel may need to install more RAM in his computer.

1 ....

2 ....

[2]

[Total 4 marks]

3 When a computer is switched on the BIOS runs. The BIOS is stored in the computer's ROM.

a) State **two** functions of the BIOS.

1 ....

2 ....

[2]

b) Explain why the BIOS is stored in ROM instead of RAM.

....

....

[2]

When many programs are running at once a computer may have to use virtual memory.

c) Explain how virtual memory works.

....

....

[2]

d) Explain **one** disadvantage of using virtual memory.

....

....

[2]

[Total 8 marks]

CPU and System Performance

1 Mary works as a graphic designer. For her latest project, she plans to upgrade her computer in order to run design software more smoothly.

Identify **three** components that could be upgraded to improve the performance of her computer.

1 ....

2 ....

3 ....

[Total 3 marks]

2 Jackson is considering upgrading his PC. Will offers to sell his old CPU to Jackson. Will's CPU is the same type as Jackson's CPU but has a different specification.

Jackson's CPU
8 cores
6 MB cache
1.6 GHz clock speed

Will's CPU
4 cores
3 MB cache
2.8 GHz clock speed

a) Define the term clock speed.

    ....
    [1]

b) Explain why using a CPU with a large cache capacity may increase CPU performance.

    ....

    ....
    [2]

c) Do you think Jackson should buy Will's CPU? Give reasons to justify your decision.

    ....

    ....

    ....

    ....
    [4]

d) Jackson decides to increase the RAM in his PC from 4 GB to 8 GB.
   He was disappointed to find no noticeable increase in his computer's performance.
   Explain why this may be the case.

    ....

    ....
    [2]

    [Total 9 marks]

Secondary Storage

Match each sentence to the correct storage device.

Suitcase

Hard Disk Drive

Magnetic Tape

Has different formats such as CD.

Data is stored on a stack of magnetic disks.

Usually comes on a reel in a cassette.

Stores clothes for when you go on holiday.

Floppy Disk

Solid State Drive

Optical Disc

1 Shaun is going on a two week skiing trip. Each night, he will copy photos and videos to his laptop's secondary storage.

a) Give **three** characteristics to consider when choosing a suitable type of secondary storage for a computer system.

1 ....

2 ....

3 ....

[3]

b) Shaun will be using a helmet-mounted action camera to record videos whilst skiing. The camera records video onto a solid state memory card.

i) Give **two** reasons why solid state storage is suitable for an action camera.

1 ....

2 ....

[2]

ii) Explain why a hard disk would be an unsuitable storage type for an action camera.

....

....

[2]

[Total 7 marks]

2 Caley is getting a custom-built computer. She has a choice of two options for secondary storage: A 500 GB HDD or a 128 GB SSD. For each storage option, give reasons why Caley may choose it over the other option.

500 GB HDD ....

....

128 GB SSD ....

....

[Total 4 marks]

3 Every night a large law firm backs up roughly 600 GB of data. At the end of each month, one final backup is taken and stored permanently, and the daily backups are deleted.

a) After three weeks, how much data will they have from daily backups? Give your answer in TB.

....

[1]

b) Circle a suitable storage type to store the daily backups from the choices below.

Hard Disk Drive   **Magnetic Tape**   **Solid State Drive**   **Optical Disc**

[1]

c) Outline the advantages and disadvantages of using your choice in part b) for data backups.

Advantages ....

....

Disadvantages ....

....

[4]

[Total 6 marks]

4 Jason has bought a new laptop.
The laptop contains 3 GB RAM and 128 GB secondary storage.

a) Explain why secondary storage is needed in addition to RAM.

....

....

....

....

[3]

Jason wants to back up the data on his laptop twice a week.
b) Give **two** advantages and **two** disadvantages of storing his backup data on optical discs.

Advantages 1 ....

2 ....

Disadvantages 1 ....

2 ....

[4]

[Total 7 marks]

Exam Practice Tip

Make sure you can rhyme off all the advantages and disadvantages for each type of secondary storage.
Consider the speed, capacity, cost and the various characteristics of each storage device, e.g. reliability and portability.

Systems Software

Warm-Up

Find the names of **five** operating systems below.

```
E M J R C O D E R D A I K Y S E
F L E G I M R B N Z B O V I A U
W I F M E A N D R O I D A O L M
A N T B Q C C E R I H T I S R T
R U S E H O D W I N D O W S D S
D X F U H S D G T B N I R T Z B
```

1 David has just installed a new operating system on his computer.

a) State **three** functions of an operating system.

1 ....

2 ....

3 ....

[3]

After the new OS was installed, it automatically downloaded and installed the device drivers.

b) Describe what is meant by device drivers.

....

....

[2]

[Total 5 marks]

2 Keri's operating system includes an encryption utility that helps to keep her personal data secure.

a) Describe the process of data encryption and decryption.

....

....

....

[2]

b) Identify **two** other features or utilities the operating system may provide
to help protect Keri's personal data.

1 ....

2 ....

[2]

[Total 4 marks]

3   Josephine's computer has a multi-tasking operating system. Explain how the operating system manages memory and CPU time to allow the computer to multi-task.

....

....

....

....

....

....

....

....

....

[Total 6 marks]

4   Selina has customised the graphical user interface (GUI) on her computer's operating system.

a) Describe the purpose of a graphical user interface.

....

....

[2]

b) Selina's operating system also has an optional command line interface.
   i)   Define what is meant by a command line interface.

   ....

   ....

   [1]

   ii) Identify **two** benefits of using a command line interface instead of a GUI.

   1 ....

   ....

   2 ....

   ....

   [2]

   [Total 5 marks]

Section One — Components of a Computer System

5   Annie has a three year old laptop. She is giving the laptop a full service before selling it on.

a) Annie runs some 'Disk Health' utility software to check for any problems with her HDD.

  i) Define what is meant by utility software.

  ....

  ....

  [1]

  ii) Give **two** other examples of utility software.

  1 ....

  2 ....

  [2]

b) The utility also reports that Annie's hard disk is 25% fragmented.

  i) Describe how a hard disk can become fragmented over time.

  ....

  ....

  ....

  ....

  [3]

  ii) Explain **one** problem caused by a fragmented hard disk.

  ....

  ....

  [2]

  iii) Briefly describe the defragmentation process.

  ....

  ....

  ....

  ....

  [3]

  iv) Suggest why it could be better to do the disk clean-up
       before defragmentation rather than afterwards.

  ....

  ....

  [1]

  [Total 12 marks]

Section One — Components of a Computer System

Mixed Questions

1   Hardeep wants to try a new operating system on his computer.
The new operating system is optimised for use with a touchscreen.

	Hardeep's PC	**OS Minimum Requirements**
Processor:	2.1 GHz, 4 cores	1.0 GHz, 4 cores
RAM:	2 GB	2 GB
Storage:	256 GB, 125 MB free	19 GB free space
GPU:	Integrated 256 MB	Dedicated 512 MB

a) Hardeep needs to upgrade some of the components in his computer before the new
operating system can be installed. State which components must be upgraded.

1 ....

2 ....

[2]

b) Would you recommend that Hardeep upgrades any other components in his computer?
Explain your answer.

....

....

[2]

c) Explain why an operating system requires a certain amount of RAM.

....

....

[2]

d) The new operating system's GUI is optimised for touchscreen use.
Describe **two** features that a GUI may include to take advantage of touchscreen technology.

1 ....

....

2 ....

....

[4]

e) The new operating system organises the files on Hardeep's computer into a structure of folders.
Suggest **two** other file management tasks the operating system may carry out.

1 ....

2 ....

[2]

[Total 12 marks]

2 Three computers are on sale in a computer store. Their specifications are shown below.

	CGPC3000	**XZ Monochrome**	**CGPC-Pro**
CPU	Ixoteck S44: Quad-core, 2.4 GHz, 4 MB cache	Ixoteck X3: Octa-core, 3.3 GHz, 6 MB cache	Ixoteck S30: Dual-core, 2.4 GHz, 2 MB cache
RAM	4 GB	8 GB	4 GB
Storage	1 TB HDD (5400 rpm)	500 GB SSD	128 GB HDD (7200 rpm)
Graphics	Integrated 512 MB	Ixoteck UltraBurst 2 GB	Integrated 512 MB
OS	Legacy 3	Legacy 3	Legacy 3
Price	£300	£650	£200

a) Kirstie and Liam go shopping for computers. They each have different requirements but don't want to spend more money than is necessary.

i) Kirstie needs a computer for word processing, emailing, downloading high definition TV series from an online store and basic photo editing.
Which computer would you recommend for Kirstie? Give reasons for your answer.

....

....

....

....

....

[4]

ii) Liam wants to replace his old video games console with a new gaming PC. He wants to be able to play the latest games releases, but will also need his computer for browsing the Internet, and editing databases. Which computer would you recommend for him?
Give reasons for your answer.

....

....

....

....

....

[4]

b) Kirstie also buys a printer with her new computer to print high-quality posters.
Outline how the operating system uses memory buffers when printing the posters.

....

....

[1]

[Total 9 marks]

Section One — Components of a Computer System

Units

Find the five units that measure data and order them in increasing size.

NIBBLE

HEX   BIT   PETABYTE   TIB   BYTE   KILOBYTE   BOOLEAN   MUNCH   BINARY

_____ , _____ , _____ , _____ , _____

smallest ————————————————————————————————————→ largest

---

1 Misha wants to save some music files onto a solid state drive (SSD).

a) State which SSD has the largest capacity:
250 gigabyte (GB), 200 000 megabyte (MB) or 0.3 terabyte (TB).

....
[1]

b) Calculate how many 5 MB music files Misha could save onto a 250 GB SSD.

....
[2]

[Total 3 marks]

---

2 Gigi is designing some images to be used in a video game. Each image file takes up 100 kB.

a) Calculate how many bits there are in each image file.

.... bits
[2]

b) Gigi has made 5000 image files for the game. Calculate, in GB, the total size of these files.

.... GB
[2]

c) The images are stored on her computer using binary.
Describe how binary is used to represent data in computers.

....

....
[2]

[Total 6 marks]

Binary Numbers

Black dots on the first binary clock below indicate the time 11:17:59.
Shade the dots on the second clock to show the time 15:57:40.

1   Work out these conversions.

a) Convert the 8-bit binary number 10010011 into a denary number.

....
[1]

b) Convert the denary number 252 into an 8-bit binary number.

....
[1]
[Total 2 marks]

2   An 8-bit binary addition involves adding two 8-bit numbers and getting an 8-bit answer.

a) Add the binary numbers 00111001 and 01010110.

....
[2]

b) Computers can encounter overflow when adding binary numbers.
  i)   Give an example of an 8-bit binary addition where an overflow occurs.

[2]

  ii)   Explain how a computer deals with the overflow.

....

....
[2]
[Total 6 marks]

3   Binary shifts can be used to quickly multiply and divide binary numbers.

     a) Complete a 3 place left shift on the binary number 00011010.

....

[1]

     b) State an appropriate binary shift to divide a binary number by 4 and use it on 11010100.

....

[2]

     c) Yasha says "Adding a binary number to itself is the same as a 2 place left shift."
        Is he correct? Explain your answer.

....

....

[2]

[Total 5 marks]

4   In a video game, every 8-bit binary number represents a unique magic word or a spell.
     The last digit determines if it is a magic word (0) or a spell (1).

     a) State how many unique magic words there are.

....

[1]

Spells are made by adding the binary numbers of words together and then adding 00000001.
Overflow bits are ignored. A sample of spells and words are shown below.

Number	Word
00110100	Shazam
01010000	Abra
01100110	Kadabra
10011100	Hocus
11001010	Pocus

Number	Spell
00100011	Teleport
01101111	Fireball
10110111	Blizzard
11110001	Zap
11111111	Earthquake

Because the last digit is always O, this is the same as changing the least significant bit from a O to a 1.

     b) What spell is made with the words 'Abra' and 'Kadabra'?

....

[2]

     c) Identify **two** words from the table that could have been used to make the Earthquake spell.

.... and ....

[2]

[Total 5 marks]

Exam Practice Tip

If you end up with too many bits after some 8-bit binary arithmetic and don't know what to do you could be giving away some easy marks! Make sure you use the technical term for this, **overflow**, and can explain it clearly.

Section Two — Data Representation

Hexadecimal Numbers

Fill in the boxes below to complete the hexadecimal equations.

A + ☐ = C   6 + ☐ = E   ☐ + 6 = C   F + ☐ = 1E

---

1 Work out these hexadecimal problems.

Remember — no calculators allowed.

a) What is the largest denary number that can be made using 2 hex characters?

....
[1]

b) Convert the hexadecimal number 37 into denary.

....
[2]

c) Convert the denary number 45 into hexadecimal.

....
[2]
[Total 5 marks]

---

2 A security program encrypts passwords using a hexadecimal conversion.

The binary code of each letter for the password 'CAT' is shown below.

01000011   01000001   01010100

a) Convert each binary number above to a hexadecimal number to encrypt the password 'CAT'.

....
[3]

b) The password 'DOG' is encrypted as 44 4F 47.
   i)   Convert the first encrypted letter to binary.

....
[1]

   ii) What password would be encrypted as 43 4F 44 45?

Hint: Look back at previous question parts.

....
[2]
[Total 6 marks]

3 Work out the following hexadecimal calculations by first converting into denary.
Give your answers in denary.

a) A + C

....

[2]

b) 2B – F

....

[2]

c) 28 + 14 – A

....

[3]

[Total 7 marks]

4 Daniel is a programmer. He makes the following two claims about hex numbers.

Claim 1: "Hex is much easier to work with than binary."

Claim 2: "Converting from denary to hex is easier than converting from binary to hex."

Would other programmers agree with Daniel's claims? Explain your answers.

Claim 1: ....

....

....

Claim 2: ....

....

....

[Total 4 marks]

5 Show that the hexadecimal equation 10 + 25 + 3A = 6F is correct.

Start by converting each number on the left hand side to denary.

....

....

....

....

[Total 4 marks]

Characters

1   Helena is writing a news article using a word processor.

a) Define the term 'character set'.

....

....

[1]

b) Helena presses a key on her keyboard, and her monitor displays a character.
   Describe how the computer recognises the character she enters.

....

....

....

[2]

[Total 3 marks]

2   The table on the right shows information on two standard character sets.

Character Set	Bit Length
ASCII	8
Unicode®	32

a) i)   Describe in general how the bit length affects the size of the character set.

....

....

[1]

ii)   Ed claims that Unicode® can represent 4 times as many characters as ASCII.
     Is he correct? Explain your answer.

....

....

[2]

b) Suggest **two** benefits of using Unicode® to encode each character.

Benefit 1: ....

Benefit 2: ....

[2]

c) In ASCII, the character q is represented by the binary code 0111 0001.
   What binary code represents the letter t?

The next character in the alphabet is one binary value greater than the previous character.

....

[1]

[Total 6 marks]

Storing Images

1 A computer screen displays images using pixels.

a) Describe how the number of bits used per pixel affects the colours in an image.

....

....

[2]

b) How many bits per pixel would be needed for a pattern that uses 256 unique colours?

....

[1]

c) Explain which of the following images would need
the greatest number of bits to represent all of the pixels.

> 1 bit is needed to
> represent either O
> (white) or 1 (black).

Image 1   Image 2   Image 3

....

....

....

[4]

[Total 7 marks]

2 An image has a colour depth of 32 bits and an image resolution of 200 × 100.

a) i) Define the term 'image resolution'.

....

[1]

ii) Calculate the file size, in bits, of this image.

.... bits

[2]

b) Explain how decreasing the image resolution would affect the quality of the image.

....

....

[2]

c) Explain the purpose of metadata in an image file.

....

....

[2]

[Total 7 marks]

Storing Sound

1   A two-second clip of analogue sound is being sampled to be stored in a digital format.

a) Describe the process of sound sampling.

....

....

....

....

[3]

Remember, 5 Hz means 5 samples per second.

b) Add crosses to the graph above to show where
   samples would be taken if the sample rate was 5 Hz.

[2]

[Total 5 marks]

2   Jade has made two recordings of herself reading an extract from a novel to use in an audiobook.
    The duration, sample rate and bit depth of each recording are shown below.

	Duration	Sample Rate	Bit Depth
Recording 1	102 seconds	20 000 Hz	4 bits
Recording 2	100 seconds	50 000 Hz	8 bits

a) Explain which recording you would expect to have better sound quality.

....

....

[2]

b) Calculate the file size, in bits, of recording 2.

.... bits

[2]

c) Give **one** drawback of using recording 2 rather than recording 1 for the audiobook.

....

[1]

[Total 5 marks]

Compression

	Lossless	Lossy
MP3		✔
FLAC	✔	

1   Ashmita wants to listen to a podcast. The podcast is available in two file formats — MP3 and FLAC.

a) Explain why compression is used for audio files.

....

....
                                                                                                            [2]

b) Give **one** benefit and **one** drawback of downloading the FLAC file.

Benefit: ....

Drawback: ....
                                                                                                            [2]

c) Ashmita downloads the podcast to her smartphone in the MP3 format.
   Give **two** reasons why she might have done this.

1 ....

....

2 ....

....
                                                                                                            [4]
                                                                                                [Total 8 marks]

2   State and explain which type of compression would be most appropriate in these examples.

a) Uploading 100 holiday photographs to a social media account.

Type Of Compression: ....

Explanation: ....

....
                                                                                                            [2]

b) Uploading a photograph of a model for a fashion magazine.

Type Of Compression: ....

Explanation: ....

....
                                                                                                            [2]
                                                                                                [Total 4 marks]

Exam Practice Tip

It's good practice to relate your answers to the question that's being asked — if you're given an example of a person using lossy compression for an audio or image file, then it's best to answer how it will benefit **them**.
Think up some everyday examples where compression is used and how it is a benefit to the user in each case.

Section Two — Data Representation

Mixed Questions

1 A program takes a binary number as an input and outputs a hexadecimal number using the algorithm below.

- Input an 8-bit binary number.
- Complete a 2 place left shift on the binary number.
- Swap the most significant bit of the result from 0 to 1 or vice-versa.
- Convert the new binary number to a hexadecimal number and output it.

a) What is the output if 10110110 is the input?

....

[4]

b) Find an 8-bit binary number that could be an input if the output is 2C.

....

[4]

[Total 8 marks]

2 In ASCII, the binary code 01001011 represents the letter K.

a) i)   What is the binary representation of the letter M?

....

[1]

ii)   What is the hexadecimal representation of the letter P?

....

[2]

b) Unicode® also uses binary code to represent different letters. Give **one** difference between the binary representations of a character in Unicode® and in ASCII.

....

[1]

c) Assuming each character is stored using ASCII, how many bits would you need to store the following string?

`Where's the library, Abi?`

.... bits

[1]

[Total 5 marks]

3 A three hour radio broadcast transmits an analogue signal. A digital recording of the broadcast is made by sampling different points of the analogue wave.

a) Complete the table below for point x.

	x	y
Denary Value		50
Binary Value		00110010
Hexadecimal Value		32

[3]

b) Explain how increasing the sample rate can affect the quality of the sound file.

....

....

[2]

[Total 5 marks]

4 Florence is a graphic designer for a publishing company. The image editing software that she uses represents each unique colour as a six digit hexadecimal code.

A single hex character can represent 16 different values.

a) As a power of 16, how many possible unique colours could Florence use?

....

[1]

b) Explain **one** benefit to programmers of using hexadecimal codes to represent different colours.

....

....

[2]

Florence saves the same image as three different file types (shown in the table). One of the file types uses lossy compression.

File Type	JPEG	PNG	TIFF
Size	0.2 MB	1 MB	0.9 MB

c) State and explain which file type is most likely to be an example of lossy compression.

....

....

[2]

d) Evaluate the impact if Florence always used lossless compression to store all her images.

....

....

....

....

....

[6]

[Total 11 marks]

Networks — LANs and WANs

1 In an office there are six computers, a scanner and a router connected together in a Local Area Network (LAN).

a) Define the term Local Area Network (LAN).

....

[1]

b) State **three** advantages of connecting the computers together into a Local Area Network.

1 ....

2 ....

3 ....

[3]

[Total 4 marks]

2 Dishley Academy is connected to other schools in the area using a Wide Area Network (WAN).

Hint: WANs connect LANs.

a) Describe what is meant by a Wide Area Network (WAN).

....

....

[2]

b) Explain **two** of the potential benefits of using a WAN to connect the Academy to other schools.

1 ....

....

2 ....

....

[4]

c) Explain **three** factors that can affect the performance of a network.

1 ....

....

2 ....

....

3 ....

....

[6]

[Total 12 marks]

Networks — Hardware

| Warm-Up | Draw a line between the name and the matching definition. |

Bluetooth®

CAT5e cable

Coaxial cable

Fibre optic cable

Contains twisted pairs of copper wires.

A type of cable that uses light to carry signals.

A type of wireless technology.

A type of copper cable that consists of a central wire protected by a metal shield.

1 Jane works from home. She connects her laptop and television to her home Local Area Network (LAN). Jane uses a home router to connect her LAN together.

a) State the name of the hardware device inside the laptop that connects it to the LAN.

....

[1]

b) Jane can connect her devices to the router using either Ethernet or Wi-Fi®.

i) State how an Ethernet connection is different to a Wi-Fi® connection.

....

[1]

ii) Jane's television lacks any wireless capability. State the name of the hardware Jane can use to allow her television to connect to the LAN wirelessly.

....

[1]

c) Jane's home router functions as a switch, router and Wireless Access Point (WAP) all in one. Outline the function of each of these devices.

i) Switch

....

....

[2]

ii) Router

....

....

[2]

iii) Wireless Access Point (WAP)

....

....

[2]

[Total 9 marks]

Client-Server and Peer-to-Peer Networks

Warm-Up

Put the numbers 1 to 5 in each of the boxes below
to show the correct order of a Client-Server request.

☐ The web server sends the web page data to the web browser.

☐ The web server processes the request.

☐ The web browser displays the web page for the user to view.

☐ The user clicks on a web page link in their web browser.

☐ The web browser asks the web server to send the web page data.

1 Bill's graphic design business has ten members of staff, each with their own computer. The staff work together by sharing files between their computers.

a) The staff's computers are connected together in a Peer-to-Peer (P2P) network.

i) Describe what is meant by a Peer-to-Peer (P2P) network.

....

....
[2]

ii) Identify **two** benefits and **two** drawbacks of using a Peer-to-Peer (P2P) network.

Benefits 1 ....

2 ....

Drawbacks 1 ....

2 ....
[4]

b) An IT consultant suggests the company should adopt a Client-Server network setup.

i) Describe what is meant by a Client-Server network.

....

....
[2]

ii) Identify **two** benefits and **two** drawbacks of changing from a Peer-to-Peer (P2P) network to a Client-Server network.

Benefits 1 ....

2 ....

Drawbacks 1 ....

2 ....
[4]

[Total 12 marks]

Network Topologies

1   A leisure centre has a Local Area Network (LAN) consisting of five computers and a central server connected in a star topology.

a) Draw a diagram of the leisure centre's star network.

[2]

b) Identify **three** advantages of the star topology.

1 ....

2 ....

3 ....

[3]

[Total 5 marks]

2   The table below shows star topologies, partial mesh topologies and full mesh topologies for different numbers of nodes.

Nodes are the dots on the diagrams used to represent network devices.

a) Complete the table by correctly connecting the nodes in the white cells.

Number of nodes	Star	Partial Mesh	Full Mesh
4	Switch		
5	Switch		
6			

[4]

b) Explain **one** advantage and **one** disadvantage of mesh topologies compared to star topologies.

Advantage ....

....

Disadvantage ....

....

[4]

[Total 8 marks]

3   A company has its employees' computers spread across four floors. The computers on each floor are connected to that floor's server in a star network. Employees need to access files on all of the servers, so each of the four servers are connected in another star network, with a central switch located on the ground floor.

It might help to sketch the network like a traditional star diagram. Start with the switch in the middle, then draw the servers as the four nodes connected to it. Finally, draw three nodes coming off each of the servers.

a) Describe the effect of the failure of the central switch on the rest of the network.

....

....

[2]

b) The company decides to remove the switch from the network and instead connect the four servers in a full mesh network, as shown in this diagram.

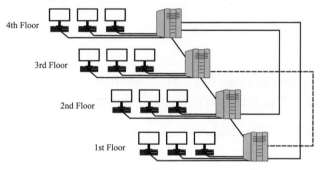

Explain the advantages and disadvantages to the company of connecting the servers together in a full mesh network instead of a star network.

....

....

....

....

....

[4]

[Total 6 marks]

Exam Practice Tip

Make sure you get to grips with what each different network topology looks like. Remember: a full mesh is when <u>all</u> devices are directly connected to each other, while devices in a partial mesh are only indirectly connected.

Network Protocols

1   When data is sent over the Internet, it follows certain network protocols.

a) Define the term network protocol.

....

[1]

b) The table below shows the names and functions of different network protocols.
Complete the missing spaces in the table.

Protocol	Function
TCP	
	Responsible for directing data packets across a network.
FTP	
SMTP	
	Used to retrieve emails from a server. The user downloads a copy of the email and the server holds the original email until the user deletes it.
	Used to retrieve emails from a server. The server holds the email until the user downloads it, at which point the server deletes it.

[6]

[Total 7 marks]

2   Sally works in an office. Her computer has a MAC address, which helps Sally to access files from the company's server.

a) Describe what is meant by a MAC address.

....

....

[2]

b) The network managers at Sally's company work with layers of network protocols.
   i)   Describe what is meant by a layer of network protocols.

....

....

[2]

   ii) Identify **three** benefits of using layers when working with network protocols.

   1 ....

   2 ....

   3 ....

[3]

[Total 7 marks]

Networks — The Internet

1   The Internet offers access to a variety of services, including the World Wide Web.

a) Explain the difference between the Internet and the World Wide Web.

....

....

[2]

b) State the function of a Domain Name Server (DNS).

....

[1]

c) Explain why devices need IP addresses to connect to the Internet.

....

....

[2]

[Total 5 marks]

2   A magazine publishing company based in rural Scotland connect their computers in a LAN using a Client-Server setup. Their writers live elsewhere in the UK and either email or post their articles to the company, where they are edited in time for the weekly deadline.

a) A manager suggests that they use a cloud-based setup instead.
   Give **two** services that the cloud can provide.

1 ....

2 ....

[2]

b) Suggest **one** advantage and **one** disadvantage to the company of changing
   from their current system to one which uses the cloud.

Advantage: ....

....

Disadvantage: ....

....

[2]

[Total 4 marks]

Network Security Threats

Warm-Up

Draw lines between the type of malware and its description.

Ransomware	Alters permissions and access levels on the user's device.
Virus	Tells the user their computer is infected with malware in order to make them follow malicious links to "fix" the problem.
Rootkit	Self-replicating malware.
Spyware	Secretly monitors user actions.
Trojan	Encrypts the data on the user's device, making them pay money to the hacker in exchange for the key to decrypt it.
Scareware	Spread by users copying infected files.
Worm	Malware disguised as legitimate software.

1   National Lending Bank stores the banking data of thousands of customers. The bank has recently suffered a passive attack, where customer data was stolen, and a denial-of-service attack.

a) i)   Define the term passive attack.

....

[1]

ii) State **one** way of preventing a passive attack.

....

[1]

b) Explain what is meant by a denial-of-service attack.

....

....

[2]

c) As a result of recent attacks, the bank is planning to carry out a pentest on the network. Explain how pentesting is used to improve network security.

....

....

[2]

[Total 6 marks]

2 Hannah regularly receives fake emails claiming to be from well-known banks and other organisations.

These types of emails are a form of social engineering.

a) State the name given to the practice of sending fake or spoof emails.

....

[1]

b) Explain the purpose of these fake emails.

....

....

[2]

c) Hannah also receives suspicious emails that contain attachments, sometimes from names in her own contacts list. Explain the dangers of opening untrusted email attachments.

....

....

[2]

[Total 5 marks]

3 Kate is a network administrator at a secondary school. She has put in place measures to prevent attacks on the school's network, including firewalls and different user access levels.

a) Explain how a firewall can prevent attacks on the school's network.

....

....

[2]

b) Explain why the school's network needs to have different user access levels.

....

....

....

[3]

c) A hacker recently broke through the school's network security using a brute force attack.
   i)   Explain what is meant by a brute force attack.

....

....

[2]

   ii) Identify **two** steps the school can take to protect against a brute force attack.

   1 ....

   2 ....

[2]

[Total 9 marks]

Section Three — Networks

4 A supermarket sells its products online. It stores user account information in a database which is accessed when the customer places an order. The supermarket recently suffered a security breach in which the data of thousands of customers was stolen.

a) A common way for databases to be breached is through SQL injection.

i) Explain how SQL injection works.

....

....
[2]

ii) Explain how SQL injection attacks can be prevented.

....

....
[2]

b) The supermarket believes the data was stolen through social engineering.
Describe an example of how the thieves could have used social engineering to steal the data.

....

....
[2]

[Total 6 marks]

5 A law firm has 100 members of staff in an office building in London.
The firm stores confidential data about its clients on a server.

Discuss the security methods that the law firm could use to protect the data against network threats.

> You should consider the threats posed to the firm's network and how they could be prevented.

....

....

....

....

....

....

....

....

....

....
[Total 8 marks]

Exam Practice Tip

Out there in the real world it's not enough to name types of attacks — you need to know how to prevent them as well. The same is true of the exam — for every possible threat you can think of, keep in mind a prevention method for it too.

Mixed Questions

1   A Yorkshire-based television company has two studios, one based in Leeds and the other based in York. The company's computer network is shown in the diagram below.

Leeds — Local Area Network (LAN)   York — Local Area Network (LAN)

CAT5e cables

Wide Area Network (WAN) between the two sites using leased fibre optic cables.

Wireless Access Point (WAP)

Switch

Router   Router

The Leeds studio uses wired connections, whereas the York studio uses wireless connections.

a) Select words from the following list to complete the sentences below:

   i)   .... is a network protocol used on wired networks.

       Ethernet   **Fibre optic**   **WAP**   **Coaxial**   **Bluetooth®**

[1]

   ii)   The Leeds studio is using a .... topology.

       Bus   **Ring**   **Star**   **Mesh**

[1]

b) Describe **one** difference between a CAT5e twisted pair cable and a coaxial cable.

   ....

   ....
[2]

c) Outline the advantages and disadvantages of each LAN setup.

   The Leeds studio's wired setup:...

   ....

   ....

   The York studio's wireless setup: ....

   ....

   ....
[4]

d) Identify **one** reason why the company uses leased lines for its WAN.

   ....
[1]

[Total 9 marks]

2 A networking hardware company ensures their routers meet certain network standards.

a) What is a network standard?

....

[1]

b) Outline why it is important for the company to make routers to meet these standards.

....

....

[2]

[Total 3 marks]

3 Sinead is a college lecturer. She usually does research for her lectures on a laptop connected to her home network.

a) Sinead uses a cloud server to store any research photos that she finds. Describe the communication that takes place between the cloud server and Sinead's laptop when she downloads one of these photos.

....

....

[2]

b) While researching on the Internet, Sinead notices that some website addresses have HTTP before them and some have HTTPS before them. Explain what is meant by each one, including why some websites use one instead of the other.

....

....

....

....

[3]

c) Sinead often takes her laptop into the college and connects it to the college's wireless LAN. Describe a potential network security threat that this could create.

....

....

[2]

d) Explain **one** security measure that the college might take to reduce the risks posed by users like Sinead connecting devices to the network.

....

....

....

[2]

[Total 9 marks]

Section Three — Networks

Ethical and Cultural Issues

Tick one box in each row to show whether it concerns censorship or surveillance.

	Censorship	Surveillance
A business monitors what their employees view online.		
A country's government blocks access to Facebook®.		
A government agency intercepts emails containing certain words.		
A school restricts access to harmful websites.		
An Internet Service Provider collects data on browsing habits.		

1   A supermarket replaces all of their staffed checkouts with electronic self-service checkouts that provide a faster service. The owners of the supermarket notice an increase in profits, but employees who work on the checkouts lose their jobs.

For each group of people below, state whether the supermarket's decision would affect them positively or negatively, giving a reason for your answer.

Owners of the supermarket

The effect on this group was: Positive / Negative

Reason: ....

Employees

The effect on this group was: Positive / Negative

Reason: ....

Customers

The effect on this group was: Positive / Negative

Reason: ....

[Total 3 marks]

2   Identify **two** health risks caused by using technology. State how each could be prevented.

Health risk: ....

Prevention: ....

Health risk: ....

Prevention: ....

[Total 4 marks]

3 Jasmine uses several social media websites.
Jasmine was a recent victim of cyberbullying.

a) Define the terms cyberbullying and trolling.

Cyberbullying: ....

Trolling: ....

[2]

b) Suggest **two** reasons why cyberbullying and trolling have become a problem on social media.

1 ....

2 ....

[2]

c) Describe **one** example of how social media can affect the privacy of those who use it.

....

....

[2]

d) Social media has also had a positive impact on how we communicate.
Describe **one** way in which social media benefits its users.

....

....

[2]

[Total 8 marks]

4 Some businesses restrict and monitor what their employees view online.

a) Discuss the impact of the increasing use of censorship software in the workplace.

....

....

....

....

[4]

b) Discuss the ethical issues of employers monitoring what their employees are viewing online.

....

....

....

....

[4]

[Total 8 marks]

5 Tom works for a smartphone company. Tom is stressed because he feels he can never switch off from work.

a) Explain how new technology could have allowed work to intrude into other areas of Tom's life.

....

....
[2]

b) Tom's company releases a new smartphone every year.
Outline the social pressures that can be created by the regular release of new technology.

....

....
[2]

c) Tom's neighbour, Jerry, is stressed because he is finding it difficult to apply for jobs. All the companies he wants to apply to only accept online applications, and he has limited access to the Internet. Explain **one** reason why somebody might only have a limited access to the Internet.

....

....
[2]
[Total 6 marks]

6 In many factories robots have replaced humans for routine tasks such as cutting and joining materials together and retrieving products stored in a warehouse.

Discuss the impact of robots replacing humans to carry out routine tasks in factories.

In your answer you might consider the impact on: factory staff, technology and ethical issues.

....

....

....

....

....

....

....

....
[Total 8 marks]

Exam Practice Tip
There's rarely a right or wrong answer to these issues, so expect the exam to use them in longer discussion questions, not just knowledge testing. These high mark questions will often give a real-life situation. When you're backing up points with examples or evidence, make sure it's all relevant to the situation you're given — so don't write about killer intelligent toasters unless the situation you're given is about the threats of using AI in kitchen appliances...

Environmental Issues

| Warm-Up | Circle the words below that are the names of materials used in electronic devices. |

Jupiter   Plastic   Mercury   Silver

Platinum   Potato   Gold

Copper   Cedar wood   Mithril   Fancyshinyinium

1   Modern devices contain a range of different raw materials.

a) Define the term raw material.

....

[1]

b) Identify **two** effects that the use of raw materials for electronic devices has on the environment.

1 ....

2 ....

[2]

[Total 3 marks]

2   The average smartphone is only used for two years before it is discarded as e-waste.

a) Define the term e-waste.

....

[1]

b) Identify **two** reasons why smartphones are only used for a
short amount of time before they are discarded.

1 ....

2 ....

[2]

c) Outline the problems that the short life span of many electronic devices has on the environment.

....

....

....

....

[4]

d) Outline how the problem of e-waste can be managed to limit its impact on the environment.

....

....

[2]

[Total 9 marks]

3 The average household can spend almost £100 a year on wasted electricity.

a) Identify **two** ways that electronic devices waste electricity.

1 ....

2 ....

[2]

b) Explain how hardware manufacturers can limit the amount of electricity wasted by electronic devices.

....

....

[2]

c) Briefly discuss the challenges in meeting the increasing worldwide demand for electricity.

....

....

....

....

[4]

[Total 8 marks]

4 Shaun has had his computer monitor for two years and it still works. He would like to throw away the monitor and replace it with a new, more energy efficient model.

Think about Shaun's decision in terms of energy, e-waste and natural resources.

Discuss the environmental impact of Shaun's decision to replace his current monitor with one which is more energy efficient.

....

....

....

....

....

....

....

....

[Total 8 marks]

Exam Practice Tip

It's useful to remember that almost everything has some sort of environmental effect. Take a look at question 6 on page 41 — using robots in the workplace has a load of environmental impacts on top of all the ethical issues. Some questions might even ask about both ethical and environmental issues, so try to get used to writing about them together.

Computer Legislation

Warm-Up

Draw a line between each issue and the law that it would apply to.

A hospital holds the medical records of its patients so they can be treated.

A criminal hacks into a broadband company's network and steals its customers' account details.

A company is found to be using unlicensed software on all of their work computers.

A polling company holds data on members of the public for a survey it is conducting.

An employee accesses their manager's network account and deletes company data.

Computer Misuse Act 1990

Data Protection Act 2018

Copyright, Designs and Patents Act 1988

---

1   The Data Protection Act 2018 gives rights to data subjects.

a) Define the term data subject.

....

[1]

b) One of the principles of the Data Protection Act is that data must be accurate and kept up to date. State **three** other principles of the Data Protection Act.

1 ....

2 ....

3 ....

[3]

c) i)   Felix believes an organisation is holding some of his personal data.
        Outline the rights that Felix has regarding accessing his data.

....

....

[1]

ii) Give a scenario where access to his data may be denied.

....

....

[1]

[Total 6 marks]

2 Hayley is creating a website with information on her local town and its sports teams.

a) Define the term copyright.

....

[1]

b) Hayley wishes to use a photograph that she has found on another website. The image has been copyrighted. Outline what Hayley needs to do if she wishes to use the photograph legally.

....

....

....

....

[3]

[Total 4 marks]

3 A cinema collects information from customers who book seats to watch movies. The cinema would like to store this information for the following reasons:
   • to make it easier for customers when they book seats in the future.
   • to enable the cinema to contact customers with details of future films.

Explain the measures that the cinema should take to ensure that customer data is stored legally.

....

....

....

....

....

....

....

....

....

....

[Total 6 marks]

Exam Practice Tip

For the longer questions, don't just write down everything you know about that topic — all the points you make should be directly relevant to the question. Planning your answer or jotting down a few notes beforehand can help you with this. The question may even suggest points for you to cover — use them to make sure you're answering the question.

Open Source and Proprietary Software

1   A marketing company has the same, paid-for, proprietary software on all of its computers.
     The software provides facilities for word processing, presentations, spreadsheets and databases.

   a) Describe what is meant by proprietary software.

   ....

   ....
   [2]

   b) Identify **two** advantages and **two** disadvantages to the company of using proprietary software.

   Advantages 1 ....

   2 ....

   Disadvantages 1 ....

   2 ....
   [4]

   [Total 6 marks]

2   WeynTeck sells a product called a TV-PC.
     TV-PCs plug into any USB-compatible TV, and come
     packaged with a selection of open source software.

   TV-PC *Only £39.99!* NEW
   Turn your TV into a PC for
   word processing, spreadsheets,
   slideshows, databases and photos!
   Includes portable projector-keyboard
   — type on any surface!

   a) Describe what is meant by open source software.

   ....

   ....
   [2]

   b) Explain **one** advantage and **one** disadvantage to WeynTeck
      of using open source software on the TV-PCs.

   Advantage ....

   ....

   Disadvantage ....

   ....
   [4]

   [Total 6 marks]

Mixed Questions

1   Satellite navigation systems are used by many car and lorry
    drivers to enable them to plan and follow a route to their destination.

Discuss the impact of the increasing use of satellite navigation systems
to plan journeys. In your answer you might consider the impact on:
car and lorry drivers, technology, ethical issues and environmental issues.

....

....

....

....

....

....

....

....

....

....

[Total 8 marks]

2   Many people today use social media to communicate with their friends.

Discuss the impact of the use of social media to communicate and share information. In your answer
you might consider the impact on: technology, ethical issues, privacy issues and cultural issues.

....

....

....

....

....

....

....

....

....

....

[Total 8 marks]

3   Smartphones can now be used instead of notes,
coins or bank cards when making purchases in a shop.

Discuss the impact of the increasing use of smartphones as a replacement to
traditional forms of payment. In your answer you might consider the impact on:
customers and shop owners, technology, ethical issues and environmental issues.

....

....

....

....

....

....

....

....

....

....

[Total 8 marks]

4   Recent years have seen the increasing use of computer technology
to distribute and view digital media content (music, movies and books).

Discuss the impact of the increasing use of digital media. In your answer you might consider
the impact on: consumers and businesses, technology, environmental issues and legal issues.

....

....

....

....

....

....

....

....

....

....

[Total 8 marks]

Computational Thinking

Use the correct words to complete the sentences below.

solving
complex
abstraction
important
details
information
individually

Decomposition is breaking down a ....complex......... problem into smaller problems and .... each one ....

.... is picking out the .... bits of .... from the problem, ignoring the specific .... that don't matter.

1   A hardware company plans to make a computer keyboard for Greek language students.

a) Complete the missing rows in the table below to show the decomposition and abstraction steps the hardware company might take when making the keyboard.

Decomposition	Abstraction	
Things to look at	**Details to ignore**	**Details to focus on**
What keys are needed?	Letters from other alphabets.	Letters from the Greek alphabet.

[4]

b) Define what is meant by algorithmic thinking.

....

[1]

[Total 5 marks]

2   A file uploading service won't allow two files with the same file name to be uploaded. If a file name already exists, it will ask the user to change the file name.

a) Describe with examples how abstraction can help decide how to compare the files.

....

....

....

[3]

b) Describe with examples how decomposition could be used to help program this task.

....

....

....

[3]

[Total 6 marks]

Writing Algorithms

Warm-Up

Cross out the commands that don't go with the flowchart symbol.

Input / Process   Sub program / Stop   Decision / Start   Process / Output

1 Bernard has written the algorithm on the right using pseudocode.

```
input height
input width
area = height × width
output area
```

a) Define what is meant by an 'algorithm'.

....

....

[1]

b) Describe what Bernard's algorithm does.

> Go through the pseudocode line by line and describe what each bit does.

....

....

....

[3]

c) State the value of `area` if `height = 5` and `width = 10`.

....

[1]

[Total 5 marks]

2 A courier company allows customers to track the delivery of parcels.
To track a specific parcel, customers enter an eight-digit parcel number.

Complete the pseudocode below that checks whether a customer has entered a valid parcel number.
The pseudocode should:
- Ask the user to enter a parcel number.
- Output "Valid parcel number" if there are eight characters.
- Output "Not a valid parcel number" if there are not eight characters.

input ....

if .... then

....

else

....

endif

[Total 4 marks]

3 The flowchart below shows how to convert miles to kilometres.

INPUT miles → kilometres = miles × 8/5 → OUTPUT kilometres

a) Identify **one** problem with this flowchart.

....
[1]

b) State the distance in kilometres of 10 miles.

.... km
[1]

c) Refine the flowchart to do the following:
- Use a more accurate conversion factor of 1.6093 instead of 8/5.
- Ask the user if they wish to convert another distance.
  If they do, perform the new calculation, otherwise, the flowchart ends.

[5]
[Total 7 marks]

4 At Tom's Tombola, every ticket number ending in either a 5 or a 0 is a winning ticket.

a) Complete the flowchart below to show a ticket number as an input
and whether it is a winning ticket as an output.

Start → INPUT ticketNumber

[4]

The flowchart in part a) can be represented by this sub program: | ticket |

b) Use | ticket | to draw a second flowchart for someone picking 10 tickets.

[6]
[Total 10 marks]

5   A robot moves on the 4 × 4 square grid shown below.
    A sub program, SqMove, is part of a flowchart that tells the robot how to move.

Draw a flowchart to show how the robot moves. The flowchart should:
  • Ask the user to enter which square the robot starts on.
  • Run the sub program SqMove in a loop.
  • Stop when the robot reaches the top or the right of the grid.

This is when x = 4 or y = 4

[Total 6 marks]

6   A garden centre is having a sale. New customers get £5 off for items costing £50 or more.
    Existing customers get a discount based on the stock level of the item, as shown below.

Stock Level	0 – 9	10 – 99	100 +
Price Reduction	0 %	10 %	20 %

a) Draw a flowchart to calculate the cost of an item using the information above.

[6]

b) A wheelbarrow costs £100 and 110 are in stock.
   Use your flowchart to find how much one wheelbarrow would cost an existing customer.

£ ....

[1]

[Total 7 marks]

Exam Practice Tip

Unless a question says otherwise, when asked to write an algorithm you have the option of using pseudocode or a flowchart. Don't get too caught up on the wording of your algorithm but make sure that it is clear and easy to interpret.

Search Algorithms

1 Nicola has a list of numbers: 2, 3, 7, 5, 13, 11.

a) She says, "I can't use a binary search to find 13." Why is this the case?

....

[1]

b) Show the steps of a linear search to find 13 in the list above.

[2]

[Total 3 marks]

2 Sonia has a sorted list of ice cream flavours that she sells in her shop.

a) Show the stages of a binary search to find the word 'butterscotch' in the list below.

butterscotch	chocolate	mint	strawberry	vanilla

[4]

b) Give **one** advantage of using a binary search over a linear search.

....

....

[1]

c) Six more flavours are added to Sonia's list. The list is still in alphabetical order.
Explain why it would only take two iterations of a binary search to find the ninth item in the list.

....

....

....

....

[3]

[Total 8 marks]

Section Five — Algorithms

Sorting Algorithms

1   Use the insertion sort algorithm to put these European cities into alphabetical order.

Riga	Paris	Oslo	Baku	Minsk

[Total 4 marks]

2   Six athletes compete in a long jump competition. Their best jumps are shown below.

5.32 m	5.50 m	5.39 m	6.50 m	6.28 m	6.14 m

Show the stages of a bubble sort to list these jumps in order from shortest to longest.

[Total 4 marks]

3   Kim has a hand of playing cards, all of the same suit: 3, 7, 6, 2, 5.

a) Arrange the cards in order from highest to lowest using:

i)   An insertion sort.   ii)   A merge sort.

[4]   *[4]*

b) Explain **one** benefit of using an insertion sort over a merge sort on a computer.

....

....

[2]

[Total 10 marks]

4 The list below shows the calorie content of different packets of sweets.

450	350	230	180	650	500	340	270

a) Show the stages of a merge sort to arrange the list from lowest to highest.

[4]

b) Give a reason why the merge sort:

i) Splits the list into single items.

....

[1]

ii) Uses ordered lists at each merging step.

....

[1]

[Total 6 marks]

5 The code on the right performs a sorting algorithm on an array called `items`.

```
array items[5]
items = [4, 2, 1, 8, 6]
sorted = false
while sorted == false
    sorted = true
    for i = 0 to 3
        if items[i] > items[i + 1] then
            x = items[i]
            items[i] = items[i + 1]
            items[i + 1] = x
            sorted = false
        endif
    next i
endwhile
```

This code is written in OCR Exam Reference Language — it's covered in Section 6.

a) Explain what the code inside the FOR loop does.

....

....

....

....

[2]

b) Explain what will cause the algorithm to stop.

....

....

....

[3]

c) Identify the sorting algorithm that the code represents.

....

[1]

[Total 6 marks]

Exam Practice Tip

Sorting algorithms can be lengthy, but don't miss out any steps — make sure you show **every** stage of the algorithm in the exam. This way the examiner knows you clearly understand the algorithm and can reward you some easy marks.

Mixed Questions

1   Mike is posting an online advert on a forum to promote his band's upcoming tour.

a) Outline **one** decomposition and a matching abstraction process when creating the advert.

Decomposition: ....

....

Abstraction: ....

....

[2]

b) The algorithm on the right shows how the cost (in £) of an advert for basic and premium forum users is calculated.

What is the difference in cost between a basic and a premium user?

```
cost = 5.0
user = input("Premium or basic?")
if user == "premium" then
    cost = cost * 0.5
else
    cost = cost + 1.0
endif
output cost
```

£......................

[2]

[Total 4 marks]

2   Every 5 minutes, an app on a mobile phone records the electrical current (in mA) passing through a pair of connected headphones.

A sample of the readings is shown below.

10 mA	15 mA	12 mA	18 mA	20 mA

a) Show the stages of a linear search to find the value '12 mA' in the list above.

[2]

b) If a reading is greater than 30 mA the mobile phone will buzz and then the program will stop. If not, the program will wait 5 minutes before taking another reading. Draw a flowchart to show this program.

Your flowchart should show an iteration — a loop that repeats the task.

[6]

[Total 8 marks]

Section Five — Algorithms

3 Leigh has a list of six gymnastics apparatus.

Floor	Pommel	Rings	Vault	Parallel Bars	High Bar

a) Show the stages of a merge sort to list the apparatus into alphabetical order.

[4]

b) Show the stages of a binary search to find 'Rings' from your ordered list above.

[4]

[Total 8 marks]

---

4 Mr Spencer is playing a board game which uses two 4-sided dice. The table shows what a player will score depending on which numbers the two dice land on. * means have another roll.

		Dice 1			
		1	**2**	**3**	**4**
Dice 2	**1**	0	*	0	*
	2	*	4	*	6
	3	0	*	0	*
	4	*	6	*	8

> Use this table to work out the rules for scoring — look at how odd and even dice rolls affect the scores.

a) Draw a flowchart to show how to **play** and **score** this game.

[6]

b) Each score is stored in a list. At the end of the game the list is searched to see if an 8 was scored. Tick the most suitable search algorithm for this task and explain your answer.

Binary Search ☐   Linear Search ☐

....

[2]

[Total 8 marks]

Section Five — Algorithms

Section Six — Programming

Programming Basics

Warm-Up

Circle the items that would be best represented using an integer data type:

The nickname of your best friend.

The weight of one potato in kg.

The number on a rolled dice.

An email address.

The number of people on a football pitch.

The age of a pet in whole months.

The length of a car to the nearest metre.

1 A bakery stores data about the pies it makes.

Complete the table below by giving the most appropriate data type for each bit of information.

Information	Example	Data Type
Flavour	Apple and Strawberry	
Weight (kg)	1.35	
Quantity in stock	7	
Gluten-free?	False	

[Total 4 marks]

2 State what the code will do in each of the following:

a) `int("76423")`

....

[1]

b) `ASC(T)`

....

[1]

c) `12 MOD 5`

....

[1]

[Total 3 marks]

3 A pedestrian crossing uses a button to request the traffic to stop.

Tick the data type you would use to record whether the button has been pressed or not and give a reason for your answer.

Data Type	Tick (✓) one box
Real	
Boolean	
String	

Explanation: ....

....

[Total 2 marks]

4 A teacher writes the following program to analyse the test scores of a pupil. Line 03 is missing.

```
01 x = input("Enter mark for test 1")
02 y = input("Enter mark for test 2")
03
04 print(z)
```

Complete line 03 so that the program:
a) Calculates the total score of the pupil.

....

[1]

b) Calculates if their score in test 1 is greater than or equal to their score on test 2.

....

[1]

c) Calculates the pupil's combined score from both tests as a percentage out of 160 marks available.

To find the percentage, divide the total marks the pupil got by the total number of marks available and multiply by 100.

....

[1]

[Total 3 marks]

5 A petrol station needs a program to calculate the cost of fuel for each customer.

a) Identify appropriate data types for:
   i) The name of the fuel that the customer used.

....

[1]

   ii) The total cost of the customer's fuel.

....

[1]

b) Explain why it's important to use the correct data type to store information.

....

....

....

[2]

c) Describe with an example how the function str() might be used when printing the receipt.

....

....

....

[2]

[Total 6 marks]

Exam Practice Tip

Questions about data types are usually a great way to pick up a few easy marks in your exam, so it's really important that you know the names of the different data types and the best situation to use each one. As for the different operators — they'll crop up all the way through your exam so commit them to memory now so you don't come unstuck.

Constants and Variables

1   The program below calculates the cost of a burger in pounds at a fast food restaurant.
A standard burger costs £6.50 with additional costs for toppings and eating in the restaurant.

```
const standard = 6.5
toppings = 0
eatIn = false
toppings = input("How many toppings?")
eatIn = input("Are they eating in?")
if eatIn == "Yes" then
    print(standard + 0.5*toppings + 1)
else
    print(standard + 0.5*toppings)
endif
```

a) List **all** the variables in this program.

....

[2]

b) How much extra does it cost to eat your burger
inside the restaurant?

....

[1]

c) The restaurant manager says that 0.5 should have been declared as a constant.
Give **two** reasons for declaring this value as a constant.

1 ....

2 ....

[2]

[Total 5 marks]

2   The program below calculates the value of an investment at the end of one year.

Identify **two** problems with the constants or variables in this program.

```
const investment = input("Enter investment.")
rate = "0.2"
for x = 1 to 12
    interest = rate * investment
    investment = investment + interest
next x
print(investment)
```

1 ....

....

2 ....

....

[Total 2 marks]

3   Jeremiah is writing a program for a gym where customers need to scan their
gym card to get in and out. The program should keep track of how many
people are in the gym and refuse entry once the gym is at maximum capacity.

Describe **one** constant and **two** variables that the program could use.
For each one explain why it should be a constant or variable.

Constant ....

....

Variable 1 ....

....

Variable 2 ....

....

[Total 6 marks]

Strings

Given that animal = "lobster", draw lines to match each of these string methods with the correct output.

animal.length	bst
animal.right(3)	7
animal.upper	LOBSTER
animal.subString(2, 3)	ter

1   A digital radio stores the current date as a string under the variable name date.
The radio is broken and is stuck on the date: 8 January 2016

State the output from each of the following pieces of code:

a) date.length

....
[1]

b) date.left(1) + date.subString(10, 4)

....
[1]

c) date.subString(2, 3).upper

....
[1]

[Total 3 marks]

2   A juice company generates a product ID for each of its fruit juices. The product ID is
generated using string concatenation on the first three letters of the fruit (in uppercase)
and the volume of fruit juice in ml. E.g. a 500 ml carton of apple juice would be APP500.

a) Define what is meant by string concatenation.

....
[1]

b) What would the product code be for a 2000 ml carton of orange juice?

....
[1]

c) Complete the algorithm below so that line 03 reassigns the uppercase name of the fruit
to the fruit variable and line 04 assigns the final product ID to the prodID variable.

```
01 fruit = input("Enter the name of the fruit.")
02 volume = input("Enter the volume of the juice.")

03 fruit = ........................................................................................................

04 prodID = ......................................................................................................
05 print(prodID)
```

[3]

[Total 5 marks]

Program Flow

Put each of these statements into the correct box below.

IF-THEN-ELSE   SWITCH   DO UNTIL   IF-ELSEIF   WHILE

Selection Statements	Iteration Statements

1   Jasminda has written the following program to convert minutes into hours and minutes.

```
minutes = input("Enter a number of minutes.")
hours = minutes DIV 60
mins = minutes MOD 60
print(str(hours) + " hours and " + str(mins) + " minutes")
```

a) Which programming construct has been used in this program?
   Tick the correct box.

   Sequence ☐   Selection ☐   Iteration ☐

   [1]

b) What would the program print if the input was 150?

   ....

   [1]

   [Total 2 marks]

2   Salik needs a program that will ask users to create a password and then check if the
     password contains at least six characters. If it contains fewer than six characters
     the user must try again, otherwise the user is informed that their password is valid.

     Write an appropriate program for Salik.

     You may want to consider using a
     DO UNTIL loop in your program.

     [Total 3 marks]

3 An electric heater has three temperature settings (1, 2 and 3).
The code below controls the temperature of the heater.

```
setting = input()
if setting == "3" then
    temperature = 50
elseif setting == "2" then
    temperature = 30
elseif setting == "1" then
    temperature = 20
else
    temperature = 0
endif
```

a) Refine this program to use a SWITCH statement.

[3]

b) Give **two** reasons why a SWITCH statement is appropriate for this program.

1 ....

2 ....

[2]

[Total 5 marks]

4 In a basketball arcade game a player gets 10 shots to score as many baskets as they can. The code on the right keeps track of a player's score.

```
score = 0
basket = false
for x = 1 to 10
    basket = input("Did they score?")
    if basket == true then
        score = score + 1
    endif
next x
print(score)
```

a) What is the data type of the variable `basket`?

....

[1]

b) Explain why a count-controlled loop has been used instead of a condition-controlled loop.

....

....

[2]

c) The third line of code is replaced with 'for x = 1 to 10 step 0.5'.
State what effect this will have on the game.

....

....

[1]

d) Another basketball game gives the player an unlimited amount of shots until they've scored 5 baskets. Explain why a condition-controlled loop would be more appropriate for this game.

....

....

[2]

[Total 6 marks]

5   Joanne wants a program that will print a sentence she has typed once the sentence is finished. The sentence will be finished when Joanne types a full stop, question mark or exclamation mark (".", "?" or "!").

Use the variables `keypress` and `sentence` to write a suitable program for Joanne.

You must use either:
- OCR Exam Reference Language, **or**
- a high-level programming language that you have studied.

[Total 5 marks]

6   Karl and John are playing snap. Write a program that:
- Asks for the name of the winner of each game.
- After ten games checks who has won more and displays the winner's name or tells them that it's a draw.

You must use either:
- OCR Exam Reference Language, **or**
- a high-level programming language that you have studied.

[Total 6 marks]

Exam Practice Tip

When it comes to writing programs and algorithms in the exam it's important that you remember to lay them out correctly — this means using indentation and finishing statements, e.g. with endif or endswitch. Another key thing to remember is to use == when you mean "is equal to" and = as the assignment operator — otherwise you'll lose marks.

Boolean Logic

Circle all of the Boolean expressions that are true.

12 > 4 AND 5 == 5   12 <= 4 OR 10 != 5   7 >= 3 AND 91 > 99

NOT(11 == 3)   9 == 8 OR 2 > 16   NOT(9 > 4 AND 5 < 2)

1   Two truth tables are given below. A and B are inputs. P and Q are outputs.

Draw the correct logic gates for each of these truth tables.

a)

A	P
0	1
1	0

[1]

b)

A	B	Q
0	0	0
0	1	1
1	0	1
1	1	1

[1]

[Total 2 marks]

2   A logic gate can be written as P = A AND B.

a) State the value of input B when input A is 1 and output P is 0.

B = ...
[1]

b) A NOT logic gate is placed after the AND logic gate to make the logic diagram below.
State the input values when output P is 0.

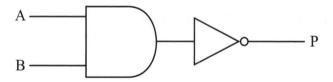

A = ... B = ...
[1]

[Total 2 marks]

3   A garden centre has a climate monitoring system that gives warnings if the temperature and humidity aren't at suitable levels. The climate monitoring system contains this algorithm.

```
if humidity == 50 AND (temperature > 16 AND temperature < 25) then
    print("Humidity and temperature at acceptable levels.")
elseif temperature <= 16 OR temperature >= 25 then
    print("Warning — Please alter the temperature.")
else
    print("Warning — Please alter the humidity.")
endif
```

a) What will the output be if humidity = 30 and temperature = 16?

....

[1]

b) What will the output be if humidity = 30 and temperature = 20?

....

[1]

[Total 2 marks]

4 Ollie writes a truth table for the logic circuit Q = A OR (NOT B).

a) Complete his truth table below.

'True' and 'False' can be thought of as 1s and 0s.

A	B	Q
FALSE	FALSE	TRUE
FALSE	TRUE	
	FALSE	
TRUE		

[3]

b) Ollie draws the following logic diagram for Q = A OR (NOT B).
   Annotate the diagram to show **two** things that are incorrect.

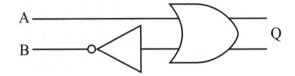

[2]

[Total 5 marks]

5 A car uses a logic circuit to decide whether to start the engine or not.
   • The car has two buttons, labelled **S** (START) and **D** (DRIVE).
     If both buttons are on, the engine will start.
   • The engine also starts if the ignition switch **I** is turned on.

a) Draw the logic circuit diagram for this system, with **Z** as an output.

[3]

b) Write a Boolean expression for this logic circuit.

....

[1]

c) State all possible values of the inputs and outputs if:
   i)   Button D is on but the car doesn't start.

....

[1]

   ii) Buttons I and S are both on.

....

....

[2]

[Total 7 marks]

6   A series of transistors make the two-level logic circuit (NOT A) AND (B AND C).

a) Complete the truth table below.

A	B	C	NOT A	B AND C	(NOT A) AND (B AND C)
0	0	0			
0	0	1			
0	1	0			
0	1	1			
1	0	0			
1	0	1			
1	1	0			
1	1	1			

[3]

b) Draw the logic diagram that represents (NOT A) AND (B AND C).

[3]

[Total 6 marks]

7   A car park barrier will only open if the driver inserts a paid ticket or a valid permit.
Write an algorithm using the boolean variables `barrierUp`, `ticketPaid` and `permitValid`
that will check the status of a driver's ticket or permit before opening the barrier.

[Total 3 marks]

8   A tumble dryer will only be allowed to start if all of the following conditions are met:
  • the real variable `weight` is more than 1.5 and less than 15.0
  • the boolean variable `doorClosed` is true.

Write an algorithm that checks these conditions before allowing the tumble dryer to start.

[Total 3 marks]

Section Six — Programming

Random Number Generation

Circle all of the values that could be generated by `random(3, 8)`.

1	4	−6	7	5.5	3	'seven'	6
8.2	2.5	0	'three'	8		5	true

1 Adam wants to write an algorithm to randomise which type of tea he should drink each morning.

The types of tea below are stored in an array called `teaTypes`.

ginger	chamomile	chai	mango	lemon

Write some program code to randomly select a tea from the array and output a suitable message.

Use the random() function to generate a random number.

[Total 3 marks]

2 Many computer games use random number generation. For example, a fantasy game might use random numbers to determine a treasure chest reward.

a) Give **two** reasons why a developer might want to use random numbers in a computer game.

1 ....

2 ....

[2]

b) A developer has written the following code as part of a card game app. It is used to show 5 random playing cards from a standard deck (which is stored in an array called `deck`):

```
for x = 1 to 5
    randNum = random(0, 51)
    drawnCard = deck[randNum]
    print(drawnCard)
next x
```

Explain **one** problem with the way this code uses random number generation to draw cards.

....

....

....

[2]

[Total 4 marks]

Arrays

1   The top 5 high scores in an arcade game are stored in the `highscores` array shown below.

	0	1	2	3	4
Score	510 000	453 000	442 000	440 500	429 000

a) State the output if this code is run: `print(highscores[3])`

....

[1]

b) State the output if this code is run: `print(highscores[0] - highscores[4])`

....

[1]

c) A player's score is temporarily stored as the integer variable `newScore`.
Complete the pseudocode to check whether the `highscores` array should be updated or not.

   if .... then

      Update the array.

   endif

[2]

[Total 4 marks]

2   Kerry owns a cupcake shop which sells three different flavours of cupcake every day.

a) Write some program code that will create a one-dimensional array of size 3 called `cupcakes`,
then prompt the user to input the three flavours being sold today.

> Remember to declare the array before trying to assign values to each position.

[3]

b) Write a line of code to output the second item in the list.

....

[1]

c) Briefly describe how you could refine a line of your code from part a)
to automatically set the first element in the array to be "Raspberry".

....

....

[1]

[Total 5 marks]

3 A 2D array is used to store the names of the top 3 pupils in each event of a sports day.

a) What data type should each element of the array be assigned?

....

[1]

b) Give **three** reasons for using a 2D array to store this data.

1 ....

2 ....

3 ....

[3]

[Total 4 marks]

4 John and three of his friends are training to run a marathon. John records how many miles he and three friends ran each day last week. John stores the data in a 2D array called `distanceRun`.

		Days of the week						
		0	**1**	**2**	**3**	**4**	**5**	**6**
Runner	**0**	9	10	8	12	0	6	9
	1	10	12	15	15	0	0	10
	2	15	14	13	16	0	8	9
	3	6	8	9	10	12	12	0

The distance run on day 0 by runner 2 is given by `distanceRun[0, 2]`.
a) Write the code to display the distance run on day 4 by runner 3.

....

[1]

b) Write an algorithm that takes a runner number as an input and outputs the total number of miles that they ran over the week.

[4]

c) John has written the function `milesConvert()` which takes a distance in miles and returns the equivalent distance in km. E.g. `milesConvert(5)` would return 8. Write an algorithm to convert all distances in the array to km.

[3]

[Total 8 marks]

Section Six — Programming

File Handling

1 Frances has written a list of jobs she has to do and stored it in the ToDoList.txt file shown on the right.

> 1. Clean my room.
> 2. Computer Science homework.
> 3. Organise my stamp collection.

a) Describe what each line of the code below does.

```
01 myList = open("ToDoList.txt")
02 print(myList.readLine())
03 myList.close()
```

Line 01 ....

Line 02 ....

Line 03 ....

[3]

Frances writes the following code to replace the first job on her list.

```
myList = open("ToDoList.txt")
myList.writeLine("1. Make lunch for parents.")
myList.close()
```

b) Explain why the code Frances has written will not work as intended.

....

....

....

[2]

[Total 5 marks]

2 Omar has written an adventure story in the file adventure.txt.

Write some program code that allows a user to print Omar's adventure story one line at a time.
- Each time the user presses the "y" key the next line of the story should be printed.
- The program should end when it's at the end of the text file.

> You'll need to use the endOfFile() command.

[Total 5 marks]

Storing and Searching Data

1   Harry wants to use records to store information about the animals at his local zoo.

Complete the table below to show the most suitable data type for each field of Harry's records.

Field	Example	Data Type
AnimalType	Giraffe	
NumberOfAnimals	5	
AverageWeight	1200.2	
OriginContinent	Africa	
MeatEater	False	

[Total 5 marks]

2   The cars table below shows some data on the used cars that a car dealership has in stock.

CarID	Registration	Make	Type	Price	EngineSize
1	NF09 APY	Stanton	Hatchback	2500	1.4
2	SZ15 LUY	Fenwick	Saloon	4800	1.8
3	FQ55 ALW	Stanton	Hatchback	1700	2.1
4	SQ57 TTW	Fenwick	Estate	2300	2.8
5	NZ12 MBE	Stanton	Saloon	5200	1.8

a) How many records does this table have?

....

[1]

b) Explain the difference between a record and a field.

....

....

....

[2]

c) Draw tables showing what would be returned by each of the following SQL commands:

i) `SELECT Registration, Make FROM cars WHERE Price < 2500`

Registration	Make
....	....
....	....

[2]

ii) `SELECT Make, Type FROM cars WHERE EngineSize = 1.8`

[2]

[Total 7 marks]

3 Some of the records in a school's database are shown in the `classes` table on the right. It stores the surname, year group and form of every pupil in the school.

Surname	Year Group	Form
Simpson	10	A
Gleeson	11	C
Kane	9	B
Stoodley	11	C
Lewis	10	A
Simpson	10	A

a) What data type should be used for the "Surname" field?

....
[1]

b) Give **two** reasons why it is useful to store pupil data in records.

1 ....

2 ....
[2]

c) Describe what the following SQL query will return.
```
SELECT * FROM classes WHERE Year Group = 10
```

....

....
[2]

[Total 5 marks]

4 A comic book shop stores information about each of its comics in records. The table below shows two records stored in the `comics` table.

ID Number	Title	Publication Date	Length	Genre	Rating
0001	Hike of Hope	04-05-2019	82	Adventure	5
0002	Voyage of Destiny	05-09-2019	65	Science Fiction	4

a) Explain why the comic book shop has chosen to store this information in records rather than an array.

....

....
[2]

b) Write an SQL query to return:
  i) the rating of the Hike of Hope comic.

  ....
  [2]

  ii) the titles of all Science Fiction comics.

  ....
  [2]

  iii) the titles and lengths of all the comics that have fewer than 50 pages.

  ....
  [2]

[Total 8 marks]

Section Six — Programming

Sub Programs

1 Write a function that takes an integer as a parameter and returns the difference between the integer's cube and its square.

[Total 3 marks]

2 Isabel is developing a stopwatch application to be used on her smartphone.

a) Give **three** benefits that sub programs will bring to Isabel's application.

1 ....

2 ....

3 ....
[3]

b) Give **one** difference between a function and a procedure.

....
[1]
[Total 4 marks]

3 Noel has written the function rollTwo(n), which simulates the outcome of two random rolls of an n-sided dice, returning the results as an array. E.g. rollTwo(6) might return [5, 3].

a) Noel has declared a local variable inside the function.
Explain **two** reasons why it is good practice to use local variables.

1 ....

....

2 ....

....
[4]

b) Noel wants to use his function to simulate a game where two identical dice are rolled together.
   • The player can choose the number of sides that the dice have.
   • The player's score is the number of rolls it takes until both dice land on the same number.

Write a sub program that takes the number of sides of the dice as a parameter, uses the rollTwo function to simulate a game, and returns a player's score.

[5]
[Total 9 marks]

4 Lenny is writing a program for an exercise bike that adjusts the difficulty depending on information about the user.

a) One of Lenny's sub programs takes `weight` as a parameter.

i) Define what is meant by a parameter.

....

[1]

ii) What is the scope of a parameter?

....

[1]

b) The code on the right appears near the start of Lenny's program.

```
global difficulty = 0
currentWeight = input("Enter weight.")
procedure setInitialDifficulty(weight)
   difficulty = weight DIV 6
endprocedure
```

i) Explain what the first line of this code does.

....

....

[2]

ii) Describe what the `setInitialDifficulty` procedure does.

....

....

[2]

c) Lenny wants a sub program that adjusts the difficulty depending on the user's heart rate.

- If their heart rate is below 90 then the difficulty level should be increased by 1.
- If their heart rate is over 140 then the difficulty level should be decreased by 1.
- If their heart rate is over 160 then the difficulty level should be set to 0 and the warning message "Slow Down!" should appear.

Write a sub program that takes heart rate as a parameter and adjusts the difficulty level as stated above.

[4]
[Total 10 marks]

Exam Practice Tip

A good way to approach "Write a sub program to..." questions is by writing down the parameters you want to put in and the values you want to get out of the sub program. If you simply want to carry out a set of step-by-step instructions then a procedure is the sub program for you, but if you want to return a value then you'll need a function.

Mixed Questions

1   A microwave has three settings to control its power output:
Defrost (200W), Medium (650W) or High (900W). The name of the
setting and power output are shown on the microwave's digital display.

a) Complete the table showing what data type should be used to store these variables.

Variable	Example	Data Type
setting	Defrost	
power	200	

[2]

b) Write some program code that checks the setting variable, then changes the power output
and updates the setting and power on the digital display (or displays an error if an invalid value
of setting is used).

> The digital display shows
> e.g "Defrost 200W".

[5]

[Total 7 marks]

2   A sat nav uses the sub program shown
on the right to calculate the average
speed of a car during a journey.

```
function averageSpeed(distance, time)
    if distance > 0 AND time > 0 then
        speed = distance / time
    else
        speed = 0.0
    endif
    return speed
endfunction
```

a) What value will be returned from averageSpeed(110.0, 2.0)?

....

[1]

b) The one dimensional array, journeySpeeds, stores the average speeds of the last 10 journeys,
with the most recent journey being stored in position 0. Write a sub program that takes
the average speed from a new journey as a parameter and updates the journeySpeeds array.

> Update the last element of the
> array first to avoid losing data.

[4]

[Total 5 marks]

3 The Prime Koalas are a band consisting of four members:
John on guitar, Paul on bass, Cheryl on vocals and Ida on drums.

a) Complete the code below to generate a 2D array containing
the names and instruments of all the band members.

```
array primeKoalas[4, 2]
primeKoalas[0, 0] = "John"
primeKoalas[1, 0] = "Paul"
primeKoalas[2, 0] = "Cheryl"
primeKoalas[3, 0] = "Ida"
```

[2]

b) John wants to create a new text file called musicians.txt and write to it.
Each line of the file should contain a different band member and their instrument.
Write an algorithm that creates a new text file, then uses your array from part a)
to write this information to it.

[4]

c) Explain **two** advantages of storing data in a text file instead of in an array.

1 ....

....

2 ....

....

[4]

d) The sub program toSpeech() takes a string as a parameter, turns the string into audio data and
reads it out loud. Write a procedure using toSpeech() that takes a file name as a parameter
and reads out all the data in the file.

[5]

[Total 15 marks]

Structured Programming

1 Jessica has written the program on the right to calculate the area of any triangle with a base length less than 20.

```
num1 = input("Enter a base length")
num2 = input("Enter a height")
if num1 < 20 then
num3 = (num1 * num2) / 2
print(num3)
else
print("Base length too long.")
endif
```

Describe with an example how Jessica can use each of the following to improve the maintainability of her code.

Indentation ....

....

....

Comments ....

....

Variable names ....

....

[Total 6 marks]

2 Malcolm is leading a team who are designing a program to manage a movie streaming service. He has decomposed the program into modules, as shown on the structure diagram below.

```
                    Movie Streaming
                       Service
                          |
              ┌───────────┤
          Add New User
              |
     ┌────────┼────────────┐
Collect Username,   Add User    Send Email
Password and Email  to Database  Confirmation
```

a) Add a module named 'Add New Film' to the structure diagram above.
Include **two** examples of smaller tasks within this module.

[3]

b) Decomposing the program into modules helps to improve its maintainability.
Explain **two** other ways that the team could improve the maintainability of the program.

1 ....

....

2 ....

....

[4]

[Total 7 marks]

Defensive Design

1 A retailer keeps a database of its loyalty card holders. The retailer stores the following data for each loyalty card holder: name, age, postcode and customer number.

Name	Age	Postcode	Customer No.
Carol Foreman	20	NE85 3TW	100278
Peter Taylor	55	HA55 8PZ	223327

a) Define the term input validation.

....

....

[1]

b) Give **two** suitable input validation checks for an entry in the age field.

Think about the type of data values that each field should take.

1 ....

2 ....

[2]

c) Give **two** suitable input validation checks for an entry in the postcode field.

1 ....

2 ....

[2]

[Total 5 marks]

2 Jane uses authentication in her program, which manages a hospital's patient records.

a) Define the term authentication.

....

....

[1]

b) Explain why Jane might want to use multiple layers of authentication in her program.

....

....

....

[2]

c) Identify **one** disadvantage of using authentication in a program.

....

....

[1]

[Total 4 marks]

Testing

Tick the statements below that are true.

Syntax errors are harder to find than logic errors. ☐

Syntax errors will prevent code from running. ☐

Using the wrong Boolean operator is a logic error. ☐

Logic errors will prevent code from running. ☐

1   Huey is designing a smartphone app. His code is currently full of syntax errors and logic errors.

a) State what is meant by a syntax error.

....
[1]

b) Describe what would happen when the code is translated if all the syntax errors were corrected but the logic errors were left unchanged.

....

....
[2]

[Total 3 marks]

2   Tiffany writes some code to check if an entered pincode is between 4 and 6 characters long.

```
pincode = input("Enter your pincode.")
if pincode.length >= 4 OR pincode.length <= 6 then
    print("Valid pincode"
else
    print("Not a valid pincode, please try again")
endif
```

a) Identify the syntax error in Tiffany's code and suggest how she could correct it.

Error ....

Correction ....
[2]

b) Identify the logic error in Tiffany's code and suggest how she could correct it.

Error ....

Correction ....
[2]

[Total 4 marks]

3 A holiday company has written a simple program to calculate the price of its group holiday packages. The program asks the user to input the group size — if the group size is smaller than two or greater than 10 the program displays an error message. If not, the price (in £s) is calculated by multiplying the group size by 50 and then adding 10.

a) Describe how the company can use a test plan to check for logic errors in the program.

....

....

....

[3]

b) Complete the test plan below by filling in the missing spaces.

Test Data	Expected Outcome	Reasons for test
groupSize = 4		
	510	
groupSize = 12		Check what happens if input too large.

[5]

[Total 8 marks]

4 Jackson is developing a program to monitor the speed at which athletes in a marathon are running.

a) Jackson would like to test his program. Define the following terms:

i) Final testing

....

....

[2]

ii) Iterative testing

....

....

[2]

b) Jackson is considering only using final testing.
Explain **one** advantage and **one** disadvantage of doing this.

Advantage ....

....

Disadvantage ....

....

[4]

[Total 8 marks]

Section Seven — Design, Testing and IDEs

Trace Tables

1   Gordon wants to write a sub program to take two positive integer inputs and work out the difference between them. He writes two different sub programs, called `diffNums` and `numDiff`, shown below.

```
function diffNums(a, b)
    while a > 0 AND b > 0
        a = a - 1
        b = b - 1
    endwhile
    return a + b
endfunction
```

```
function numDiff(a, b)
    if a > b then
        return a - b
    else
        return b - a
    endif
endfunction
```

a) Complete the trace table to show the result of `diffNums(11, 4)`.

a	b

[3]

b) Explain which sub program you think Gordon should use.

....

....

....

[2]

[Total 5 marks]

2   The procedure `test` takes an array as a parameter.

a) Complete the trace table below to show the result of `test([4, 2, 7, 1, 9])`.

k	arr[k]	x	y

```
procedure test(arr)
    x = 0
    y = 0
    for k = 0 to 4
        if arr[k] > x then
            y = x
            x = arr[k]
        elseif arr[k] > y then
            y = arr[k]
        endif
    next k
    print(x)
    print(y)
endprocedure
```

[4]

b) Explain the purpose of the procedure `test`.

....

....

....

[2]

[Total 6 marks]

Translators

1 Jeffrey has written a flight simulation game in a high-level language.

Identify **two** types of translator that can turn high-level languages into machine code, and describe the translation process for each one.

Translator 1 ....

....

....

Translator 2 ....

....

....

[Total 4 marks]

2 A company specialises in writing programs using low-level languages.

a) Identify **two** reasons why some programmers still use low-level languages.

1 ....

2 ....

[2]

b) Explain why programmers might prefer to use an assembly language over machine code.

....

....

....

[2]

[Total 4 marks]

3 Cleo is writing a program to find suitable recipes based on selected ingredients. Cleo has used a high-level programming language.

Describe **three** differences between high-level languages and low-level languages.

1 ....

....

2 ....

....

3 ....

....

[Total 6 marks]

Integrated Development Environments

Below is a sketch of the layout of a new Integrated Development Environment (IDE). In each box, briefly describe the purpose of that feature.

Code Editor	Breakpoints
Error Diagnostics	

1 Cynthia is writing code for a tablet computer application aimed at children.

a) Explain how each of the following tools in the Integrated Development Environment (IDE) could help Cynthia write her application.

Translator ....

....

Error Diagnostics ....

....

Code editor ....

....

[6]

b) Cynthia's code contains syntax errors. Outline a process that could be used to correct the syntax errors using all of the IDE tools mentioned in part a).

....

....

....

[3]

[Total 9 marks]

2 Max is writing some complex software for interactive guides in a museum. His program is producing logic errors, and he is having trouble finding where they occur.

Explain how Max can use Integrated Development Environment tools to find the logic errors.

....

....

....

....

[Total 4 marks]

Mixed Questions

1 Tony is writing a program to calculate a player's score in a dice game.
A player starts with a score of 0 and rolls a dice, numbered 1 to 6, as many times as they want. After each roll they add the number the dice lands on to their score. The aim is to get as close to 21 as possible. If you go over 21 you get a score of 0.

The flowchart below shows an initial design for his program.

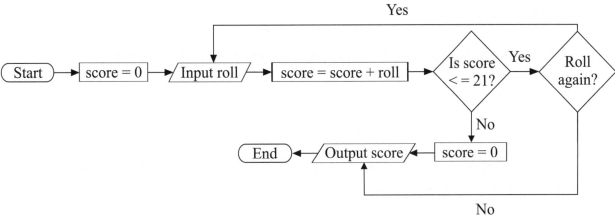

a) Tony designs a test plan for his program.
Explain why it's important for the test plan to include erroneous test data.

....

....
[2]

b) Tony tests each of the following sequences of inputs in his program.
For each test, state the type of test data, the intended outcome,
and what the actual outcome will be with his program's current design.

i) 5, 6, 4, 3, 2

Type of data ....

Intended Outcome ....

Actual Outcome ....
[3]

ii) 5, 9, 3, 2

Think about what input data Tony's program should accept.

Type of data ....

Intended Outcome ....

Actual Outcome ....
[3]

c) Identify **two** ways that Tony could use input validation in his program.

1 ....

2 ....
[2]

[Total 10 marks]

Section Seven — Design, Testing and IDEs

2 Natasha has written some code in a high-level language, which checks whether the email address the user inputs contains an "@" symbol.

```
function checkEmail(email)
    valid = false
    for x = 0 to 10
        if email.subString(x, 1) == "@" then
            valid = true
        endif
    next x
    return valid
endfunction
```

a) State **one** logic error in Natasha's code and explain why it is a logic error.

Logic error ....

Explanation ....
[2]

b) Explain **one** way Natasha could improve the maintainability of her program.

....

....
[2]

c) Explain **one** other way that Natasha could use input validation to check email addresses.

> Think about other features that all email addresses contain.

....

....
[2]

d) Natasha needs to translate her program into machine code. Outline **two** differences in the way a compiler and interpreter would translate her program.

1 ....

....

2 ....

....
[4]
[Total 10 marks]

3 An exam board is developing automated software to calculate students' final exam grades.

Evaluate the extent to which the different features of an IDE can help the exam board to develop a well-maintained program.

....

....

....

....

....

....
[Total 6 marks]

Section One — Components of a Computer System

Page 4: Computer Systems

Warm-up

RAM, hard disk drive, graphics card, optical drive, cooling fan, motherboard, heat sink.

1 a) The physical components that make up a computer system. *[1 mark]*
   E.g. RAM stick / cooling fan / mouse *[1 mark]*
   Award a mark for any correct example of hardware.

   b) The programs or applications that a computer can run. *[1 mark]*
   E.g. word processor / Internet browser / file manager *[1 mark]*
   Award a mark for any correct example of software.

2 a) A computer system built into another device. *[1 mark]*

   b) Any **two** devices, e.g.
   • Dishwasher *[1 mark]*
   • MP3 player *[1 mark]*
   • Digital thermometer *[1 mark]*
   • Washing machine *[1 mark]*
   • Manufacturing machinery *[1 mark]*
   [2 marks available in total]

   c) Any **two** benefits explained, e.g.
   • Embedded systems are far smaller than general purpose computers *[1 mark]* which means microwaves can be made more compact. *[1 mark]*
   • Embedded systems are cheaper to produce than general purpose computers *[1 mark]* which can reduce the costs / sale price of microwaves. *[1 mark]*
   • Embedded systems tend to be more reliable than general purpose computers *[1 mark]* which means that microwaves are less likely to break. *[1 mark]*
   [4 marks available in total]

Pages 5-6: The CPU

Warm-up

1 a) False *[1 mark]*
   b) True *[1 mark]*
   c) True *[1 mark]*
   d) True *[1 mark]*

2 a) Any **two** functions, e.g.
   • It follows the fetch-execute cycle. *[1 mark]*
   • It controls the flow of data within the CPU. *[1 mark]*
   • It controls the flow of data between the CPU and other parts of the computer system (such as memory, and input and output devices). *[1 mark]*
   [2 marks available in total]

   b) E.g. The ALU carries out arithmetic operations, e.g. addition, subtraction and multiplication (using repeated addition). *[1 mark]* It performs logic operations on binary data, such as AND, NOT, and OR. *[1 mark]*

   c) E.g. Cache memory is extremely fast memory in the CPU. *[1 mark]* It stores regularly used data or instructions. *[1 mark]* The CPU can access data stored in the cache much faster than retrieving it from RAM. *[1 mark]*

3 a) The registers are super fast memory that store tiny amounts of data or instructions *[1 mark]* that the CPU can access extremely quickly. *[1 mark]*

   b) The accumulator stores the results of calculations done by the ALU. *[1 mark]*
   The MAR holds any memory address about to be used by the CPU. *[1 mark]*
   The MDR holds data or instructions that have been fetched from / to be written to memory. *[1 mark]*

   c) If the program counter does not increment with each cycle, the memory address of the next instruction will always be the same, *[1 mark]* so the CPU would carry out the same instruction repeatedly. *[1 mark]*

4 E.g.
   Fetch:
   • The memory address from the program counter is copied to the MAR. *[1 mark]*
   • An instruction is fetched from memory / the address in the memory address register (MAR). *[1 mark]*
   • The fetched instruction is copied to the MDR. *[1 mark]*
   • The value in the program counter is changed to point to the address of the next instruction. *[1 mark]*
   Decode:
   • The fetched instruction is decoded by the control unit. *[1 mark]*
   • A new value may be loaded into the MAR / MDR to prepare for the execute step. *[1 mark]*
   Execute:
   • The decoded instruction is carried out / executed, *[1 mark]* e.g. data is loaded from memory / data is written to memory / a calculation is done / a program is halted. *[1 mark]*
   • The cycle is repeated. *[1 mark]*
   [6 marks available in total — fetch, decode and execute stages must all be covered for full marks.]

Page 7: Memory

1 Volatile memory is temporary memory — it requires power to retain its data content. *[1 mark]* Non-volatile memory retains its data content even when there is no power. *[1 mark]*

2 a) RAM holds any data that is currently in use, e.g. programs / OS / files / documents. *[1 mark]*
   It allows the CPU to directly access data much faster than if the data was on secondary storage. *[1 mark]*

   b) Any **two** reasons from:
   • The current amount of RAM may not meet the requirements for the software he wants to run. *[1 mark]*
   • His computer may be running slowly. *[1 mark]*
   • He may want to run more programs at once. *[1 mark]*
   • It may be constantly using virtual memory. *[1 mark]*
   [2 marks available in total]

3 a) E.g.
   • It loads the operating system. *[1 mark]*
   • It performs a variety of self-diagnostic tests on the hardware, e.g. testing RAM. *[1 mark]*
   • It checks for hardware connected to the computer. *[1 mark]*
   • It provides a basic user interface where some settings can be accessed, e.g. changing which storage device to load the OS from. *[1 mark]*
   [2 marks available in total]

   b) E.g. The BIOS must be stored in non-volatile memory, so its contents aren't lost when the computer is turned off. ROM is non-volatile memory, RAM is volatile. *[1 mark]* The contents of the BIOS should not be changed. ROM is read-only memory, but RAM is not and its contents can be altered. *[1 mark]*
   Be careful not to get non-volatile memory and ROM mixed up. ROM is just one type of non-volatile memory — there are other types of non-volatile memory that can be written to, e.g. flash memory.

c) Virtual memory is an area of secondary storage that the computer uses to store the contents of RAM temporarily *[1 mark]* when there isn't enough space in RAM to store necessary software / data. *[1 mark]* The computer will copy the items not currently in use from RAM to virtual memory, freeing up space in RAM. *[1 mark]*
[2 marks available in total]

d) E.g. Virtual memory can make a computer slow to respond, e.g. when switching between applications *[1 mark]*, because data transfer speeds from secondary storage are much slower than from RAM. *[1 mark]*

Page 8: CPU and System Performance

1 Any **three** components, e.g.
- Hard Disk Drive / secondary storage *[1 mark]*
- RAM *[1 mark]*
- CPU *[1 mark]*
- GPU *[1 mark]*
[3 marks available in total]

2 a) Clock speed is the number of instructions a CPU / processor core can carry out per second. *[1 mark]*

b) Cache is much faster than RAM. *[1 mark]* The larger the cache, the more data can be stored for quick access by the CPU, meaning the CPU should perform better. *[1 mark]*

c) E.g. Jackson's CPU has more cores than Will's CPU, which should mean better performance. *[1 mark]* It also has a larger cache than Will's, which should again lead to better CPU performance. *[1 mark]* On the other hand Will's CPU has a higher clock speed than Jackson's, so there is a chance that Will's may give better performance than Jackson's. *[1 mark]* Overall, it is hard to tell whether Will's CPU will offer better performance, therefore it seems unwise to buy Will's CPU, as it may be no better than Jackson's current one. *[1 mark]*
If you'd decided that Will's CPU was the best option, you'd still get the marks as long as you'd put together a sensible argument based on comparisons of the CPU specs.

d) E.g. Increasing the amount of RAM increases the amount of data / number of applications that the computer can hold in memory. *[1 mark]* Jackson may not use all of the current RAM in his computer, as he may use undemanding software or he may not open many programs at once *[1 mark]* so adding more RAM will not improve performance. *[1 mark]*
[2 marks available in total]

Pages 9-10: Secondary Storage

Warm-up

Has different formats such as CD — Optical Disc
Data is stored on a stack of magnetic disks — Hard Disk Drive
Usually comes on a reel in a cassette — Magnetic tape
Stores clothes for when you go on holiday — Suitcase

1 a) Any **three** characteristics from:
- Capacity *[1 mark]*
- Reliability *[1 mark]*
- Cost *[1 mark]*
- Portability *[1 mark]*
- Data transfer speed *[1 mark]*
- Durability *[1 mark]*
[3 marks available in total]

b) i) Any **two** reasons, e.g.
- Solid state storage is resistant to impacts, so is unlikely to be damaged when the action cam is in use. *[1 mark]*
- Solid state storage can be very compact and lightweight. *[1 mark]*

ii) E.g.
- Hard disks are much larger and heavier than solid state storage devices, making them unsuitable for a small, lightweight camera. *[1 mark]*
- Hard disks can be damaged greatly by impacts, so they would be unsuitable in an action camera. *[1 mark]*

2 E.g.
500 GB HDD:
- The HDD has a much greater capacity than the SSD. *[1 mark]*
- If she intends to store lots of data, e.g. photos / music / videos and 128 GB will not be enough storage space. *[1 mark]*
- The HDD is likely to cost far less per GB than the SSD. *[1 mark]*
- HDDs are said to have a longer read / write life than SSDs, so the HDD should be usable for longer. *[1 mark]*

128 GB SSD:
- The SSD will have a higher read / write speed than the HDD. *[1 mark]*
- If she needs a high performance drive for gaming the fast read / write speed may improve performance. *[1 mark]*
- If she wants the OS and programs to open and run as quickly as possible. *[1 mark]*
- The SSD will also be silent, whereas the HDD will make some noise. *[1 mark]*
[4 marks available — 2 marks for reasons to pick the HDD, 2 marks for reasons to pick the SSD]

3 a) $600 \times 7 \times 3 = 12\,600$ GB
$= 12.6$ TB *[1 mark]*

b) Magnetic tape *[1 mark]*

c) Any **two** advantages and **two** disadvantages, e.g.
Advantages:
- Magnetic tape is far cheaper per GB than other forms of secondary storage. *[1 mark]*
- Tape has a much larger data capacity than other forms of secondary storage, so is most suitable for storing many TB of data. *[1 mark]*
- Tape has a higher write speed than a HDD. *[1 mark]*

Disadvantages:
- It can take far longer to find a specific piece of data on tape, e.g. to recover certain files from a backup. *[1 mark]*
- Tape reading drives can be very expensive. *[1 mark]*
- Data can be corrupted if placed near a strong magnet. *[1 mark]*
[4 marks available in total]
Hard disk may be an acceptable answer in part b) if properly explained in part c). For example, the company would need several of them to store a month's worth of daily backups, and they are far more expensive than magnetic tapes, however they do offer some advantages over magnetic tape.

4 a) E.g.
- Secondary storage is needed to store data and software in the long term. *[1 mark]*
- Secondary storage is non-volatile memory, so retains data when there is no power. *[1 mark]*
- Computers could not function without permanent data storage, as all software and data would be lost when switched off. *[1 mark]*
- Secondary storage has a high capacity, so you can store a lot more data. *[1 mark]*
[3 marks available in total]

b) Any **two** advantages and **two** disadvantages, e.g.

Advantages:
- Optical discs have a low cost per GB. *[1 mark]*
- They are highly portable. *[1 mark]*
- They are durable against shock and water damage. *[1 mark]*

Disadvantages:
- They are very slow to write to. *[1 mark]*
- They require an optical drive to be read / written. *[1 mark]*
- They can be scratched easily. *[1 mark]*
- They have a low capacity compared to other forms of storage, e.g. flash memory cards. *[1 mark]*

[4 marks available in total]

Pages 11-13: Systems Software

Warm-up

```
E  M  J  R  C  O  D  E  R  D  A  I  K  Y  S  E
F  L  E  G  I  M  R  B  N  Z  B  O  V  I  A  U
W  I  F  M  E  A  N  D  R  O  I  D  A  O  L  M
A  N  T  B  Q  C  C  E  R  I  H  T  I  S  R  T
R  U  S  E  H  O  W  I  N  D  O  W  S  D  S
D  X  F  U  H  S  D  G  T  B  N  I  R  T  Z  B
```

1 a) Any **three** functions from:
- The OS communicates with hardware via device drivers. *[1 mark]*
- The OS provides a user interface. *[1 mark]*
- The OS provides a platform for software / applications to run. *[1 mark]*
- The OS allows a computer to multitask by controlling memory / CPU resources. *[1 mark]*
- The OS deals with file and disk management. *[1 mark]*

[3 marks available in total]

b) Device drivers are pieces of software *[1 mark]* that allow the OS and hardware to communicate with each other. *[1 mark]*

2 a) Encryption software encrypts (scrambles) the data so that it cannot be read if it is stolen. *[1 mark]* The intended reader is given the 'key' that allows them to decrypt the data and turn it back into its original form. *[1 mark]*

b) E.g.
- It may have anti-theft measures, like password or pin protection. *[1 mark]*
- It may allow different user accounts, giving each user access to their own personal data and desktop, which cannot be accessed by other users. *[1 mark]*
- It may include anti-virus software or a firewall to help protect against unauthorised users / software. *[1 mark]*

[2 marks available in total]

3 E.g.
- When applications / programs / files are opened, the OS moves the necessary parts to memory. *[1 mark]*
- The OS will remove unneeded data from memory, e.g. when programs or files are closed. *[1 mark]*
- The OS divides memory into segments. When different programs are used, their data is placed into different segments so that running applications can not write over or interfere with each other. *[1 mark]*
- The OS organises the movement of data to-and-from virtual memory. *[1 mark]*
- The OS divides CPU time between running applications / programs / processes, as it can only process one at a time. *[1 mark]*
- The OS can prioritise CPU time for different programs in order for them to be processed in the most efficient order. *[1 mark]*

[6 marks available in total — award a maximum of 4 marks for points about RAM or CPU time]

4 a) A graphical user interface allows the user to interact with the computer *[1 mark]* in a visual and intuitive way (e.g. through windows, menus and pointers). *[1 mark]*

b) i) A command line interface allows the user to interact with a computer only by typing in commands from a set list. *[1 mark]*

   ii) Any **two** benefits from:
   - Command line interfaces give greater control / more options than GUIs. *[1 mark]*
   - They are less resource heavy than GUIs. *[1 mark]*
   - They can be used to automate processes using scripts. *[1 mark]*

   [2 marks available in total]

5 a) i) Utility software is software that helps to configure, optimise or maintain a computer. *[1 mark]*

   ii) Any **two** examples of utility software, e.g.
   - Disk defragmenter *[1 mark]*
   - System diagnostic tools *[1 mark]*
   - Anti-virus / anti-spyware *[1 mark]*
   - Backup software *[1 mark]*
   - Compression software *[1 mark]*
   - File management software *[1 mark]*

   [2 marks available in total]

b) i) E.g. Fragmentation occurs when files are moved, deleted or change in size. *[1 mark]* This leaves gaps on the hard disk. *[1 mark]* Files are split into chunks to fit them into the empty spaces. *[1 mark]*

   ii) E.g. When the hard disk is fragmented, it will take longer to read / write data on the hard disk. *[1 mark]* This in turn may slow down the computer. *[1 mark]*

   iii) E.g.
   - Defragmentation software reduces fragmentation by moving files on the hard disk. *[1 mark]*
   - The empty spaces / gaps are collected together. *[1 mark]*
   - Different bits of the same file are moved to be stored together. *[1 mark]*
   - This means the read / write heads won't need to move as far across the disk, so the read / write speed should improve. *[1 mark]*

   [3 marks available in total]

   iv) E.g. Disk clean-up will remove a number of files, so it will immediately leave gaps in the data stored on the hard disk, leading to fragmentation. *[1 mark]*

Pages 14-15: Mixed Questions

1 a) Storage *[1 mark]*, GPU *[1 mark]*

b) E.g. Hardeep should upgrade the RAM in his computer, *[1 mark]* as he only just has enough RAM to cover the minimum requirements, so the OS may not run very smoothly. *[1 mark]*

It's fine to answer 'no', as long as you've justified your answer.

c) RAM stores applications and data that is currently in use. *[1 mark]* As operating systems are running all the time, a large amount of the OS is kept in RAM. *[1 mark]*

d) Any **two** features, e.g.
- Large buttons and icons *[1 mark]* that can be pressed to open applications and windows. *[1 mark]*
- Screens and menus *[1 mark]* that can be navigated / controlled by swiping or dragging with a finger. *[1 mark]*
- Support for finger gestures *[1 mark]* such as pinching to zoom out / tap and hold to open additional options / four finger swipes to swap between apps etc. *[1 mark]*
- Virtual on-screen keyboard *[1 mark]* to allow the user to type without attaching an external keyboard. *[1 mark]*

[4 marks available in total]

e) Any **two** tasks, e.g.
- Naming files *[1 mark]*
- Moving files between folders *[1 mark]*
- Creating new files *[1 mark]*
- Saving files *[1 mark]*
- Editing existing files *[1 mark]*
- Deleting files *[1 mark]*

[2 marks available in total]

2 a) i) E.g. Kirstie does not use any particularly resource-heavy software, so the XZ Monochrome would not be worth the cost. *[1 mark]* On the other hand, photo editing may benefit from using a quad-core processor instead of a dual core. *[1 mark]* As Kirstie likes to download HD TV shows, the 128 GB hard drive on the CGPC-Pro would probably be too small. *[1 mark]* Although Kirstie would benefit from a more powerful graphics card for photo editing, this gain would not be worth paying the extra £350 for. *[1 mark]* The CGPC3000 would be Kirstie's best option. *[1 mark]*

[4 marks available in total]

ii) E.g. Liam wants to be able to play the latest video games. These will be resource-heavy *[1 mark]* and require a powerful graphics card and CPU. *[1 mark]* Browsing the Internet and editing databases would be possible with all three computers, however the CGPCs would likely be too low powered for gaming. *[1 mark]* The computer with the most powerful CPU and dedicated graphics card is the XZ Monochrome, so that is Liam's best option. *[1 mark]* This may be the most expensive computer, but it is the only computer that fits his requirements. *[1 mark]*

[4 marks available in total]

There are no strictly right or wrong answers here — just make sure that you clearly explain your reasoning.

b) E.g. The OS will use memory buffers to temporarily store the image data until the printer is ready to process it. *[1 mark]*

Section Two — Data Representation

Page 16: Units

Warm-up

Bit, Nibble, Byte, Kilobyte, Petabyte

1 a) 0.3 Terabyte *[1 mark]*
1 TB = 1000 GB, 1 GB = 1000 MB. 0.3 TB = 300 GB and 200 000 MB = 200 GB, so 0.3 TB is the largest.

b) 1 GB = 1000 MB
250 GB = 250 000 MB *[1 mark]*
250 000 MB ÷ 5 MB = 50 000 *[1 mark]*

2 a) 100 kB = 100 × 1000 = 100 000 bytes *[1 mark]*
100 000 bytes = 100 000 × 8 = 800 000 bits *[1 mark]*

b) 5000 × 100 kB = 500 000 kB *[1 mark]*
500 000 kB = 500 000 ÷ 1000 = 500 MB
500 MB = 500 ÷ 1000 = 0.5 GB *[1 mark]*

c) Computers convert data into strings of 1s and 0s *[1 mark]* which are represented by electricity flowing or not flowing. *[1 mark]*

Pages 17-18: Binary Numbers

Warm-up

1 a) 147 *[1 mark]*

b) 11111100 *[1 mark]*
Draw up a table to help with binary addition and conversions.

2 a)

[2 marks available — 1 mark for correct working, 1 mark for correct answer]

b) i) Two suitable binary numbers which, when added, will cause overflow. *[1 mark]*
Correct addition of the chosen binary numbers. *[1 mark]*
E.g. 11111111 + 00000001 = 100000000 (9 bits)

ii) The computer would flag up the error *[1 mark]* and usually store the extra bits elsewhere. *[1 mark]*

3 a) 11010000 *[1 mark]*

b) A 2 place right shift *[1 mark]* gives 00110101. *[1 mark]*

c) He is not correct.
E.g. 0001 + 0001 = 0010 is a 1 place left shift.
[2 marks available — 1 mark for not correct, 1 mark for a valid explanation]

4 a) 128 *[1 mark]*
8-bit means there are 2^8 = 256 possibilities but only half of them are magic words.

b) 01010000 + 01100110 = 10110110. *[1 mark]*
Changing the last digit to a 1 gives 10110111 which is the Blizzard spell. *[1 mark]*

c) Shazam and Pocus
00110100 + 11001010 = 11111110.
Changing the last digit gives 11111111, the Earthquake spell.
[2 marks available — 1 mark for the correct answers, 1 mark for showing correct working]
The first seven digits of Shazam and Pocus have 0s and 1s in opposite places, so you can quickly work out that these add to a binary number of all 1s.

Pages 19-20: Hexadecimal Numbers

Warm-up

A + **2** = C,   6 + **8** = E,   **6** + 6 = C,   F + **F** = 1E

1   a)   255 *[1 mark]*
         FF = (16 × 15) + 15 = 255 in denary.

    b)   3 × 16 = 48 *[1 mark]*
         48 + 7 = 55 *[1 mark]*

    c)   45 ÷ 16 = 2 r 13. *[1 mark]* 13 is the remainder
         which is D in hex. So 45 is 2D in hex. *[1 mark]*

2   a)   Split bytes into nibbles and convert to hexadecimal.
         0100 = 4, 0011 = 3, so 01000011 = C = 43. *[1 mark]*
         0100 = 4, 0001 = 1, so 01000001 = A = 41. *[1 mark]*
         0101 = 5, 0100 = 4, so 01010100 = T = 54. *[1 mark]*

    b)   i)   D = 44 = 01000100 *[1 mark]*

         ii) From CAT, 43 = C and from DOG, 44 = D and 4F = O.
              E is 1 more than D (= 44) so 45 = E. *[1 mark]*
              The password is CODE. *[1 mark]*

3   a)   A = 10 and C = 12 in denary
         [1 mark for at least one correctly converted]
         So A + C = 10 + 12 = 22 *[1 mark]*

    b)   2B = (2 × 16) + 11 = 43 *[1 mark]* and F = 15
         So 2B − F = 43 − 15 = 28 *[1 mark]*

    c)   28 = (2 × 16) + 8 = 40 *[1 mark]*
         14 = (1 × 16) + 4 = 20 *[1 mark]* and A = 10
         So 28 + 14 − A = 40 + 20 − 10 = 50 *[1 mark]*

4   E.g.
    They would likely agree with claim 1. *[1 mark]*
    Hex numbers are shorter so are easier to identify, remember, edit
    and share than binary codes. *[1 mark]*
    They would likely disagree with claim 2. *[1 mark]*
    Converting binary to hex is easier than denary to hex
    — binary numbers can be split into nibbles to quickly
    read off the hex values. *[1 mark]*

5   Convert each hex number to denary: 10 = (1 × 16) = 16,
    25 = (2 × 16) + 5 = 37, 3A = (3 × 16) + A (= 10) = 58.
    Adding the denary numbers together gives 16 + 37 + 58 = 111.
    On the right hand side, convert 6F to denary: (6 × 16) + 15
    = 96 + 15 = 111. Both sides equal 111, so the equation is correct.
    *[4 marks available — 1 mark for converting any hexadecimal to
    denary, 1 mark for converting all hexadecimals on left hand side
    to denary, 1 mark for left hand side adding to 111, 1 mark for
    showing that right hand side also equals 111]*

Page 21: Characters

1   a)   A character set is a collection of characters a computer
         recognises from their binary representation. *[1 mark]*

    b)   E.g. The keyboard sends the binary code of the character to
         the computer. *[1 mark]* The code is then translated using the
         character set. *[1 mark]*

2   a)   i)   In general using more bits to represent characters
              increases the size of the character set. *[1 mark]*

         ii) He is incorrect. *[1 mark]* Unicode® could represent 2^{32}
              characters which is much more than 4×2^8. *[1 mark]*

    b)   Any **two** benefits, e.g.
         • It can support a large number of characters. *[1 mark]*
         • Can use the same character set to type in lots of different
           languages. *[1 mark]*
         • Easier for systems to operate globally. *[1 mark]*
         [2 marks available in total]

    c)   0111 0100 *[1 mark]*
         *t is 3 letters away from q, so to find the binary representation
         of t, add 3 (in binary) to q, i.e. 01110001 + 00000011.*

Page 22: Storing Images

1   a)   The number of bits per pixel determines the number of possible
         colours *[1 mark]* and so increases the amount of unique colours
         an image has available to use. *[1 mark]*

    b)   256 = 2^8, so 8 bits per pixel are needed. *[1 mark]*

    c)   In image 1, 1 bit is needed to represent each pixel (black or
         white) and there are 15 pixels. 15 × 1 = 15 bits. *[1 mark]*
         In image 2, 2 bits are needed to represent each pixel (4 different
         colours) and there are 9 pixels. 9 × 2 = 18 bits. *[1 mark]*
         In image 3, 1 bit is needed to represent each pixel and there are
         16 pixels. 16 × 1 = 16 bits. *[1 mark]*
         So image 2 requires the most bits to represent it. *[1 mark]*

2   a)   i)   The size of an image (width × height) in pixels. *[1 mark]*

         ii) 200 × 100 × 32 *[1 mark]* = 640 000 bits *[1 mark]*

    b)   A lower resolution would reduce the quality of the image
         [1 mark] because it would have fewer pixels. *[1 mark]*

    c)   Metadata is 'data about data' / information about a file.
         [1 mark] Metadata includes information about height, width,
         resolution etc. so the image is displayed properly. *[1 mark]*

Page 23: Storing Sound

1   a)   E.g. The analogue sound is recorded and input into the
         computer. *[1 mark]* The computer takes samples of the
         amplitude of the sound at specific intervals. *[1 mark]*
         These samples are then turned into binary / digital data.
         [1 mark]

    b)   1 ÷ 5 Hz = 0.2 seconds between each sample.

         *[2 marks available — 2 marks for all crosses drawn correctly,
         otherwise 1 mark for crosses drawn with a horizontal gap of
         0.2 seconds]*

2   a)   Recording 2 would have a better sound quality *[1 mark]*
         because it has a higher sample rate and bit depth, both of which
         are indications of better overall sound quality. *[1 mark]*

    b)   100 × 50 000 × 8 *[1 mark]* = 40 000 000 bits *[1 mark]*

    c)   The file size would be larger. *[1 mark]*

Page 24: Compression

1   a)   Audio files can be very large especially for long podcasts.
         Compression is used to reduce the overall size of the audio file
         [1 mark] with some acceptable loss of quality. *[1 mark]*

    b)   Any **one** benefit, e.g.
         • It will be higher quality.
         • It will match the original digital sample exactly.

         Any **one** drawback, e.g.
         • The file size will be bigger.
         • It will take longer to download.
         *[2 marks available in total — 1 mark for a correct benefit,
         1 mark for a correct drawback]*

    c)   Any **two** reasons with explanations, e.g.
         • The MP3 file will be smaller than the FLAC file *[1 mark]*
           and she may not have enough storage space on her
           smartphone for the FLAC file. *[1 mark]*
         • The MP3 file will be smaller *[1 mark]* so it would be quicker
           to download if her Internet connection is slow. *[1 mark]*
         • Not all media players support all file types. *[1 mark]*
           The media player on her smartphone may not support FLAC
           files. *[1 mark]*
         [4 marks available in total]

2 a) Any **one** compression type and relevant explanation, e.g.
   - Lossy compression *[1 mark]* — uploading is quicker as the file sizes are reduced. *[1 mark]*
   - Lossless compression *[1 mark]* — she may want to share high quality images with friends / colleagues. *[1 mark]*
   [2 marks available in total]

   b) Any **one** compression type and relevant explanation, e.g.
   - Lossy compression *[1 mark]* — a high quality JPEG file may have sufficient quality. *[1 mark]*
   - Lossless compression *[1 mark]* — an image with all original detail may be preferred so they can edit it and print it at the best possible resolution. *[1 mark]*
   [2 marks available in total]

Pages 25-26: Mixed Questions

1 a) A 2 place left shift on 10110110 is 11011000. *[1 mark]*
   Swap the most significant bit to a 0: 01011000 *[1 mark]*
   Convert 01011000 to hex by splitting into nibbles:
   0101 is 5 in hex, and 1000 is 8. *[1 mark]*
   So 01011000 is 58 as a hexadecimal. *[1 mark]*

   b) Split 2 and C and work out the binary conversion:
   2 is 0010 *[1 mark]* and C = 12 = 1100. *[1 mark]*
   So 2C is 00101100.
   Swap the most significant bit to a 1: 10101100 *[1 mark]*
   A 2 place right shift on 10101100 is 00101011. *[1 mark]*
   01101011, 10101011 and 11101011 are equally valid.

2 a) i) 01001101 *[1 mark]*
   M is 2 letters away from K so to find the binary representation of M, add 2 (in binary) to K, i.e. 01001011 + 00000010.

   ii) P = 01010000 in binary. *[1 mark]*
   Split into nibbles: 0101 is 5 and 0000 is 0 in binary.
   So P is 50 as a hexadecimal. *[1 mark]*
   P is 5 letters away from K so to find the binary representation of P, add 5 (in binary) to K, i.e. 01001011 + 00000101.

   b) The Unicode® representation can sometimes be longer because the binary representation of a character can sometimes use multiple bytes. *[1 mark]*

   c) The string contains 25 characters (including spaces and punctuation), so $25 \times 8 = 200$ bits are needed. *[1 mark]*

3 a) Denary Value = 200 *[1 mark]*
   Binary Value = 11001000 *[1 mark]*
   Hexadecimal Value = C8 *[1 mark]*

   b) Increasing the sample rate means that more samples are taken every second. *[1 mark]* The sound quality will be better as the file will more closely match the original. *[1 mark]*

4 a) 16^6 *[1 mark]*

   b) E.g. It would be easier to remember the hex code for a particular colour *[1 mark]* because the hex code would be shorter than the binary or denary equivalents. *[1 mark]*

   c) JPEG is an example of lossy compression *[1 mark]* — it produces a much smaller file size than the other formats. *[1 mark]*

   d) E.g.
   - No data is lost when compressed *[1 mark]* so graphics can be reverted back to the original — this is essential to ensure graphics are always high quality. *[1 mark]*
   - File sizes are only slightly reduced *[1 mark]* so there would be an impact on storage requirements to the company. *[1 mark]*
   - Not all software is compatible with lossless file types *[1 mark]* so clients may not be able to open graphics. *[1 mark]*
   - File sizes are large *[1 mark]* so the images will take longer to upload or attach to emails for clients. *[1 mark]*
   [6 marks available in total]

Section Three — Networks

Page 27: Networks — LANs and WANs

1 a) A group of devices connected to share data, located on a single site / over a small geographical area. *[1 mark]*

   b) Any **three** advantages, e.g.
   - The computers can share files more easily. *[1 mark]*
   - The computers can share the scanner / the computers can share hardware. *[1 mark]*
   - The business' six computers can share one Internet connection. *[1 mark]*
   - It is easier to install / update software. *[1 mark]*
   - The members of staff can communicate using instant messaging. *[1 mark]*
   - The business can store user accounts centrally. *[1 mark]*
   [3 marks available in total]

2 a) A WAN connects computers / LANs which are in different geographical locations. *[1 mark]* The communication medium is not owned by the company / the company hires the network infrastructure. *[1 mark]*

   b) Any **two** benefits with matching explanations, e.g.
   - A WAN allows the schools to share data securely *[1 mark]* meaning they can share private and sensitive data like pupil records and test scores. *[1 mark]*
   - A WAN has a dedicated amount of bandwidth *[1 mark]* meaning the schools can send large messages and files between them very quickly. *[1 mark]*
   - A WAN allows storage to be centralised at one school *[1 mark]* providing an efficient way to store and access data which is valuable to all schools without the need to duplicate files. *[1 mark]*
   [4 marks available in total]

   c) Any **three** factors with matching explanations, e.g.
   - Too many users on the network at the same time / heavy use without a sufficient amount of available bandwidth *[1 mark]* can cause congestion and slow the network. *[1 mark]*
   - Wired connections tend to improve the network performance compared to wireless connections *[1 mark]* because they are generally faster and more reliable. *[1 mark]*
   - Fibre optic cables have a greater performance capability than copper cables *[1 mark]* as the signal can travel over longer distances / the signal does not degrade / has higher bandwidth. *[1 mark]*
   - Interference from other electronic or wireless devices can affect the performance of the network *[1 mark]* by decreasing the data speed / causing the network to slow down. *[1 mark]*
   [6 marks available in total]

Page 28: Networks — Hardware

Warm-up

Bluetooth® — A type of wireless technology.
CAT5e cable — Contains twisted pairs of copper wires.
Coaxial cable — A type of copper cable that consists of a central wire protected by a metal shield.
Fibre optic cable — A type of cable that uses light to carry signals.

1) a) Network Interface Controller / Network Interface Card *[1 mark]*

   b) i) Ethernet is wired, Wi-Fi® is wireless *[1 mark]*

   ii) USB dongle / HDMI dongle / Wi-Fi® dongle *[1 mark]*

   c) i) A switch connects devices in a local area network *[1 mark]* Data is received by the switch and sent to the device with the correct MAC address. *[1 mark]*
   [2 marks available in total]

ii) A router transmits data between networks *[1 mark]* in units called packets. *[1 mark]* A router can be used to connect a local area network (LAN) to the Internet. *[1 mark]*
[2 marks available in total]

iii) A Wireless Access Point (WAP) connects devices in a local area network *[1 mark]* wirelessly / using radio waves / using Wi-Fi®. *[1 mark]*

Page 29: Client-Server and Peer-to-Peer Networks

Warm-up

1 – The user clicks on a web page link in their web browser.
2 – The web browser asks the web server to send the web page data.
3 – The web server processes the request.
4 – The web server sends the web page data to the web browser.
5 – The web browser displays the web page for the user to view.

1 a) i) A Peer-to-Peer network is a group of devices connected to share data with each other *[1 mark]* in which all devices are equal / connected without a server. *[1 mark]*

   ii) Any **two** benefits, e.g.
   • The network is easy to maintain / no specialist knowledge is required to manage the network. *[1 mark]*
   • No extra expensive hardware is required to set up the network. *[1 mark]*
   • There is no dependence on a server / the network is not dependent on any one machine. *[1 mark]*
   Any **two** drawbacks, e.g.
   • Software needs to be installed / updated on individual machines rather than centrally. *[1 mark]*
   • Copying files from one peer computer to another creates duplicate files. *[1 mark]*
   • Peer computers may slow down when other devices are accessing them. *[1 mark]*
   • Peer computers are more likely to be turned off than a server, so files cannot be accessed at all times. *[1 mark]*
   [4 marks available in total]

   b) i) A Client-Server network is a group of devices connected to a central computer (server) *[1 mark]* which manages the network / processes requests from devices (clients) / stores files centrally. *[1 mark]*

   ii) Any **two** benefits, e.g.
   • User files are stored centrally so resources are used more efficiently / files are less likely to be duplicated. *[1 mark]*
   • Software is easier to install / update because it is centrally stored. *[1 mark]*
   • Servers are more reliable than peer machines. *[1 mark]*
   • It is easier to backup data centrally. *[1 mark]*
   • There is greater security as anti-malware software can be installed centrally / user access to files can be controlled. *[1 mark]*
   Any **two** drawbacks, e.g.
   • Client-Server networks are expensive to set up. *[1 mark]*
   • The business would need to employ an IT specialist to maintain the server / network. *[1 mark]*
   • If the server fails then all the client computers lose access to their files / client computers are dependent on the server. *[1 mark]*
   [4 marks available in total]

Pages 30-31: Network Topologies

1 a) E.g.

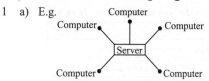

   [2 marks for a correct fully labelled diagram, otherwise 1 mark for a correct but unlabelled diagram.]

   b) Any **three** advantages, e.g.
   • If a device or connection fails the rest of the network is unaffected. *[1 mark]*
   • Direct connections to switch / server mean all devices can transmit data at once. *[1 mark]*
   • Direct connections to switch / server mean there are no data collisions. *[1 mark]*
   • It's easy to add more devices to the network compared to other topologies. *[1 mark]*
   [3 marks available in total]

2 a) E.g.

Number of nodes	Star	Partial Mesh	Full Mesh
4			
5			
6			

   [4 marks available — 1 mark for each correct diagram]
   For the partial mesh topology, you'll get the mark as long as all nodes are indirectly linked to each other and there is more than one way to get between some of the nodes.

   b) Any **one** advantage,
   E.g. If a single device or connection fails on a mesh network, the network still functions as data can go along a different route. *[1 mark]* In a star network, central switch failure will cause the whole network to fail / a single connection failure will cut that device off from the network. *[1 mark]*

   Any **one** disadvantage,
   E.g. Devices in a mesh network need many more connections than in a star network. *[1 mark]* This requires a lot of cabling which can be expensive / impractical for networks with a large number of nodes. *[1 mark]*

3 a) If the central switch fails, users will be unable to access files on other servers *[1 mark]* because there will be no connections between any of the servers. *[1 mark]*

   b) E.g.
   • Connecting servers in a mesh network means that if one connection fails, there are other routes to connect the servers. *[1 mark]* This means the network can still operate fully and all the computers can access data on all servers. *[1 mark]*
   • Adding an extra server to a mesh network would be more complicated *[1 mark]* because it would need to be connected to all of the other servers rather than just the switch. *[1 mark]*
   • Some connections would be redundant most of the time *[1 mark]* as the servers would communicate using the quickest or most direct route. *[1 mark]*
   [4 marks available in total]

Page 32: Network Protocols

1 a) A set of rules for how devices communicate. *[1 mark]*

b)

Protocol	Function
TCP	Sets rules for how devices connect on the network / splits data into packets / reassembles packets into original data / checks data is sent and delivered.
IP	Responsible for directing data packets across a network.
FTP	Used to access, edit and move files on other devices.
SMTP	Used to send emails / transfer emails between servers.
IMAP	Used to retrieve emails from a server. The user downloads a copy of the email and the server holds the original email until the user deletes it.
POP3	Used to retrieve emails from a server. The server holds the email until the user downloads it, at which point the server deletes it.

[6 marks available in total — 1 mark for each correct answer]

2 a) E.g.
- A MAC address is a unique identifier. *[1 mark]*
- A MAC address is assigned to the hardware of every network-enabled device. *[1 mark]*
- MAC addresses are used to direct data to the right device on a network. *[1 mark]*

[2 marks available in total]

b) i) A layer of network protocols is a group of protocols with similar functions *[1 mark]* that cover one particular aspect of network communications. *[1 mark]*

ii) Any **three** benefits, e.g.
- Layers break network communication into manageable pieces. *[1 mark]*
- Layers allow developers to focus on one area of the network without worrying about the others. *[1 mark]*
- Layers are self-contained. *[1 mark]*
- There are set rules for each layer. *[1 mark]*
- Layers allow interoperability / layers make companies produce compatible, universal hardware and software. *[1 mark]*

[3 marks available in total]

Page 33: Networks — The Internet

Warm up

Protocol — https
Domain name — www.cgpbooks.co.uk
Path to the specific page — secondary-books/gcse

1 a) The Internet is a global network of networks. *[1 mark]* The World Wide Web is a collection of websites hosted on web servers. *[1 mark]*

b) A Domain Name Server translates a website's domain name into its IP address / stores domain names of websites in a directory. *[1 mark]*

c) E.g. IP addresses are used to identify devices on a network / on the Internet. *[1 mark]* Routers use IP addresses to direct data packets to the correct destination. *[1 mark]*

2 a) Any two services, e.g.:
- Data storage *[1 mark]*
- Use of software/applications *[1 mark]*
- Increased processing power *[1 mark]*

[2 marks available in total]

b) Any **one** advantage, e.g.
- Users can access files from any location, so employees can share files easily. *[1 mark]*
- Cloud storage is managed by the hosting company, so may be cheaper than managing their own storage. *[1 mark]*
- The hosting company will manage the security of their data, so they do not need to spend time securing data. *[1 mark]*
- The hosting company will back up their data in the cloud, so they don't need to spend time backing up data. *[1 mark]*
- They could use cloud-based software, which will require less processing power and will be kept up-to-date. *[1 mark]*

Any **one** disadvantage, e.g.
- They will need a steady Internet connection to access the cloud services, which might be expensive. *[1 mark]*
- They are dependent on the hosting company for security, so they have little control over the security of their data. *[1 mark]*
- They are dependent on the hosting company for taking regular backups of their data. *[1 mark]*
- The cloud service may require a subscription fee, which may be more expensive in the long run than buying their own hardware and software. *[1 mark]*

[2 marks available in total]

Pages 34-36: Network Security Threats

Warm-up

Ransomware — Encrypts the data on the user's device, making them pay money to the hacker in exchange for the key to decrypt it.
Virus — Spread by users copying infected files.
Rootkit — Alters permissions and access levels on the user's device.
Spyware — Secretly monitors user actions.
Trojan — Malware disguised as legitimate software.
Scareware — Tells the user their computer is infected with malware in order to make them follow malicious links to "fix" the problem.
Worm — Self-replicating malware.

1 a) i) A passive attack is a network attack where the hacker monitors network traffic and intercepts sensitive information. *[1 mark]*

ii) E.g. Using data encryption to prevent intercepted data from being read. *[1 mark]*

b) A denial-of-service attack floods the network server / website with useless data *[1 mark]* so the user or their site visitors cannot access part of their network or website. *[1 mark]*

c) The bank can use pentesting to identify potential weaknesses in the bank's security. *[1 mark]* They'll then use this information to patch or fix the weaknesses. *[1 mark]*

2 a) Phishing *[1 mark]*

b) Phishing emails are used to trick people into thinking they are emails from legitimate organisations *[1 mark]* so that they give the criminals their personal information, e.g. account login details. *[1 mark]*

c) The email attachment could be a virus or other type of malware. *[1 mark]* Opening the attachment would therefore activate the virus or malware / cause the virus or malware to infect the device. *[1 mark]*

3 a) A firewall can stop malware and hackers from accessing the school's network *[1 mark]* by blocking traffic that is identified as suspicious. *[1 mark]*

b) E.g.
- Different user access levels prevent students from accessing the same data as teachers, including sensitive data like their peers' personal information. *[1 mark]*
- Different user access levels prevent a student from maliciously deleting or editing data. *[1 mark]*
- Different user access levels prevent students accidentally deleting or editing important files. *[1 mark]*
- Different user access levels allow network administrators to flexibly change the amount of access students and staff have to certain files. *[1 mark]*

[3 marks available in total]

c) i) A brute force attack is a type of attack on a network which uses trial and error to crack passwords *[1 mark]* by employing automated software to produce hundreds of likely combinations. *[1 mark]*

ii) Any **two** measures, e.g.
- The school can lock access to user accounts after a certain number of password attempts. *[1 mark]*
- The school can ensure that strong passwords are used / the school can ensure that passwords are long enough / the school can ensure that passwords are made of a mix of different types of character. *[1 mark]*
- The school can add additional security checks, like using a secret question or CAPTCHA test. *[1 mark]*

[2 marks available in total]

4 a) i) E.g.
- An SQL Query is entered into the input box of a website. *[1 mark]*
- The input box was not designed for that query but it is permitted by the website's / database's code. *[1 mark]*
- The inserted code runs a database query that can give unauthorised access to the whole or part of the database. *[1 mark]*

[2 marks available in total]

ii) SQL injection can be prevented by using stronger input validation *[1 mark]* so that only the intended input type will be accepted. *[1 mark]*

b) E.g.
- A criminal calls one of the supermarket's employees and pretends to be a member of the supermarket's IT team. *[1 mark]*
- The criminal gains the employee's trust through the use of jargon, information related to the supermarket or flattery. *[1 mark]*
- The criminal persuades the employee to disclose their account details, giving the criminal access to their company account. *[1 mark]*

[2 marks available in total]

5 Points you might include:

The threats posed to the firm's network
- Hackers could use rootkits, spyware and other malware to steal confidential information.
- Employees unaware of the potential dangers could be tricked into giving criminals sensitive information through social engineering.
- Disgruntled employees could use their position to attack the network, e.g. by releasing malware onto the network from a USB drive.
- Hackers with packet sniffers or other similar tools could intercept and read information entering or leaving the company's network.
- Hackers could use automated software to crack weak passwords.

Methods to ensure network security
- Automatic encryption of all data leaving and entering the network could prevent intercepted data from being read by hackers and criminals.
- Installing anti-malware and firewall software and keeping it up-to-date could prevent harmful malware from entering the network.
- Regular penetration testing to find problems in the network security.
- Educating employees on the dangers of social engineering could protect against it.
- Mandatory use of strong passwords / passwords that are changed regularly.
- Introducing an acceptable use policy that employees must sign.
- Controlling physical access to hardware / the network, e.g. using locks to prevent access to server rooms etc.
- Different user access levels given to different groups of users to limit the dangers of an attack from within the firm.

How to mark your answer:
- Two or three points with very little explanation. *[1-2 marks]*
- Three to five points with detailed explanation. *[3-5 marks]*
- Six or more detailed points that form a well-written, balanced discussion. *[6-8 marks]*

Pages 37-38: Mixed Questions

1 a) i) Ethernet is a network protocol used on wired networks. *[1 mark]*

ii) The Leeds studio is using a star topology. *[1 mark]*

b) Any **one** difference, e.g.
- CAT5e twisted pair cables use four twisted copper wires *[1 mark]* whereas coaxial cable uses one single copper wire. *[1 mark]*
- CAT5e cables prevent interference by twisting the wires together *[1 mark]* whereas coaxial cable uses a braided metallic shield to prevent interference. *[1 mark]*

[2 marks available in total]

c) E.g.
The Leeds studio's wired setup:
- Wired connections have a more reliable performance as there is no loss of signal no matter where the devices are in the building. *[1 mark]*
- Wired connections are more restrictive as it is harder to add new devices / access the network while moving through the building. *[1 mark]*

The York studio's wireless setup:
- Wireless connections are easier for the employees to connect to (e.g. no need for cables to add a laptop or mobile device to the network). *[1 mark]*
- Wireless connections can suffer from signal problems caused by building interference or interference from other wireless signals nearby. *[1 mark]*

To get all four marks, you'll need one advantage and one disadvantage for wired connections, as well as one advantage and one disadvantage for wireless connections.

d) E.g.
- Laying its own cables between Leeds and York could be too expensive for the company. *[1 mark]*
- Leased lines are likely to be more reliable and faster than other WAN connections. *[1 mark]*

[1 mark available in total]

2 a) A network standard is a set of agreed requirements for hardware and software. *[1 mark]*

b) E.g. The router will be compatible with other pieces of hardware and software *[1 mark]*, so it should be usable on most home/business networks *[1 mark]*.

3 a) E.g.
- Laptop / web browser sends a request to the cloud server, to send the photo. *[1 mark]*
- The cloud server processes the request. *[1 mark]*
- The cloud server replies with the photo. *[1 mark]*

[2 marks available in total]

b) HTTP is a protocol used to access websites and communicate with web servers. *[1 mark]* HTTPS is the secured version of HTTP where all information sent is encrypted. *[1 mark]* Websites where the user needs to enter personal information will tend to use HTTPS to keep the information secure. *[1 mark]*

c) E.g. Sinead's laptop might contain malware *[1 mark]* which could spread to the college's network, infecting other devices using the network. *[1 mark]*

d) Any security measure with explanation, e.g.
- The college could use a firewall *[1 mark]* so that any malware on user devices is stopped from spreading onto the network. *[1 mark]*
- The college could use authentication (e.g. passwords) *[1 mark]* to make sure anyone accessing the network is an authorised user. *[1 mark]*

[2 marks available in total]

Section Four — Issues

Pages 39-41: Ethical and Cultural Issues

Warm-up

	Censorship	Surveillance
A business monitors what their employees view online.		✓
A country's government blocks access to Facebook®.	✓	
A government agency intercepts emails containing certain words.		✓
A school restricts access to harmful websites.	✓	
An Internet Service Provider collects data on browsing habits.		✓

1 Owners of the supermarket — positive because they receive increased profits and do not have to pay the staff. *[1 mark]*
Employees — negative because they have lost their jobs. *[1 mark]*
Customers — positive because they receive a faster service at the checkouts. *[1 mark]*

2 Any **two** health risks, e.g.
- Eyestrain *[1 mark]* can be prevented by using suitable lighting / keeping the screen a good distance away from your eyes / taking regular breaks. *[1 mark]*
- Repetitive Strain Injury / RSI *[1 mark]* can be prevented by having a correct posture / arranging your desk appropriately / taking regular breaks. *[1 mark]*
- Back problems *[1 mark]* can be prevented by having a correct posture / using an adjustable chair / using a foot rest / using an adjustable monitor. *[1 mark]*

[4 marks available in total]

3 a) Cyberbullying: The use of social media to deliberately harm someone else. *[1 mark]*
Trolling: Causing arguments or provoking anger and frustration online. *[1 mark]*

b) Any **two** reasons, e.g.
- The Internet and social media can give people greater anonymity than they would have in real life. *[1 mark]*
- The ease of communicating online means people say things without thinking. *[1 mark]*
- There are often a lack of consequences or punishment for somebody who behaves badly online. *[1 mark]*

[2 marks available in total]

c) Any **one** example, e.g.
- Social media encourages users to share personal information and photographs with others, who may only be distant friends or colleagues *[1 mark]* so has made it more socially acceptable to share personal information. *[1 mark]*
- Social media websites have lax privacy settings by default *[1 mark]* making it difficult for users to protect their privacy. *[1 mark]*
- Users have no choice but to agree to the social media company's privacy agreement before using the website *[1 mark]* making it harder for users to control their privacy if they want to join in. *[1 mark]*

[2 marks available in total]

d) Any **one** positive impact, e.g.
- Social media allows friends to keep in touch *[1 mark]* so helps maintain or improve our social lives. *[1 mark]*
- Social media allows people to communicate with each other cheaply *[1 mark]* so there is no need to pay high phone bills. *[1 mark]*
- Social media allows you to share images and other media online quickly and easily *[1 mark]* so you do not need to invest in physical copies of media to share them with others. *[1 mark]*
- Social media allows anybody with access to the Internet the ability to express their views and opinions *[1 mark]* giving a voice to those who are often ignored. *[1 mark]*

[2 marks available in total]

4 a) E.g.
- Censoring certain websites can prevent employees from viewing harmful material, e.g. gambling, hate speech or pornography. *[1 mark]* Such material can cause harm, offense or distress to their colleagues so censoring the material helps to prevent this. *[1 mark]*
- Censoring certain websites can ensure employees are focused on their work *[1 mark]* improving the productivity for the business they are working for. *[1 mark]*
- Censoring certain websites can prevent employees from accessing illegal sites. *[1 mark]* This means the company cannot be considered legally culpable in allowing their employees to view such material. *[1 mark]*
- Censoring certain websites can infringe upon the freedom of employees *[1 mark]* as it restricts which websites they can access. *[1 mark]*
- Censorship shows the business has a lack of trust in their employees *[1 mark]* which may cause demotivation and resentment. *[1 mark]*

[4 marks available in total]

b) E.g.
- Monitoring and surveillance could restrict the freedom of employees *[1 mark]* as they may feel they cannot access certain websites. *[1 mark]*
- Monitoring and surveillance of emails and messages sent from a work computer can infringe upon employees' privacy *[1 mark]* because it means they cannot communicate with anyone confidentially / they may be using email or messaging services to send personal information to family members, doctors, etc. *[1 mark]*

- Employees may not be told about whether they are being monitored or how much of their activity is being monitored *[1 mark]* which raises issues of transparency and trust between the company and the employee. *[1 mark]*

  [4 marks available in total]

  It's important to know the different effects that censorship and surveillance can have — censorship restricts people's freedom, while surveillance damages their privacy.

5 a) E.g.
  - The Internet / social media / email mean Tom can be contacted at any time of day. *[1 mark]*
  - Tom may be expected to carry a smartphone so he can be contacted by his boss at all times. *[1 mark]*
  - Tom's smartphone may alert him when he receives work emails from clients. These can be hard to ignore. *[1 mark]*

  [2 marks available in total]

  b) E.g.
  - Companies try to influence people into using their new product, e.g. by using advertisements. *[1 mark]*
  - Many children may feel peer pressure to buy the new devices for fear of being bullied by their classmates. *[1 mark]*
  - Parents can feel pressured to buy the latest technology for their children. *[1 mark]*

  [2 marks available in total]

  c) Any **one** reason, e.g.
  - They might not have a lot of money *[1 mark]* so cannot afford to buy expensive electronic devices. *[1 mark]*
  - They might live in a rural area *[1 mark]* so could have poor network coverage. *[1 mark]*
  - They might have little knowledge of how to use the Internet or electronic devices *[1 mark]* so feel too intimidated to use them. *[1 mark]*

  [2 marks available in total]

6 Points you might include:

Factory staff
- Workers in the manufacturing sector could become unemployed, as robots take over their jobs.
- Introducing the robots could create extra jobs as people will be needed to monitor and repair them.

Technology
- The hardware and software of robots may not be sophisticated enough to fully replicate the work of human employees.
- The increased use of robots in the workplace could help improve them as problems can be identified and fixed.
- Successful use of robots in manufacturing could lead to their application in other areas of work.

Ethical issues
- Manufacturing businesses could leave hundreds of people without jobs in order to pursue profit.
- There is currently a lack of awareness of the rules on using robots in the workplace.
- By allowing robots to do the routine jobs, workers are free to do more interesting, creative and fulfilling work.
- Robots can perform hazardous tasks, meaning there could be fewer injuries in the workplace.

How to mark your answer:
- Two or three brief points with very little explanation. *[1-2 marks]*
- Three to five detailed points covering at least two of: factory staff, technology and ethical issues. *[3-5 marks]*
- Six or more detailed points that form a well-written, balanced discussion, covering all of: factory staff, technology and ethical issues. *[6-8 marks]*

Pages 42-43: Environmental Issues

Warm-up
- Plastic
- Silver
- Platinum
- Gold
- Copper
- Mercury

1 a) A material which is extracted from the earth / a material which is the basis for other products. *[1 mark]*

  b) Any **two** effects, e.g.
  - Extracting raw materials depletes scarce natural resources. *[1 mark]*
  - The process of raw material extraction causes pollution. *[1 mark]*
  - Some raw materials used in electronic devices are difficult to recycle so end up in landfill. *[1 mark]*
  - Some raw materials used in electronic devices are toxic after they are disposed of. *[1 mark]*

  [2 marks available in total]

2 a) E-waste is discarded computer material / discarded electronic material. *[1 mark]*

  b) Any **two** reasons, e.g.
  - Smartphones are portable, so can be broken easily, for example by dropping them. *[1 mark]*
  - Smartphones are not built to last more than a few years. *[1 mark]*
  - It is often cheaper to replace a smartphone than it is to repair it. *[1 mark]*
  - Smartphone manufacturers release new devices on a regular basis and use advertisements to influence people into buying them. *[1 mark]*
  - People often want to buy the newest technology and are happy to discard their old smartphones regularly. *[1 mark]*
  - Retailers only provide short warranties on many smartphones. *[1 mark]*
  - Many people feel pressured by their peers to upgrade to the latest smartphone. *[1 mark]*

  [2 marks available in total]

  c) E.g.
  - E-waste is sent to landfill sites *[1 mark]* where toxic chemicals can enter groundwater / harm wildlife. *[1 mark]*
  - The short life span of devices also means more natural resources have to be extracted to make new devices *[1 mark]* which causes pollution and depletes scarce resources. *[1 mark]*
  - Manufacturing devices uses up a lot of electricity, *[1 mark]* which is often generated using non-renewable resources. *[1 mark]*

  [4 marks available in total]

  d) E.g.
  - People can take devices to local collection facilities to be correctly disposed of according to WEEE regulations *[1 mark]* rather than throwing them out with general waste. *[1 mark]*
  - The government can put pressure on companies or local authorities to ensure WEEE regulations are being followed. *[1 mark]* The government can set recycling targets to increase the amount of e-waste that is recycled. *[1 mark]*
  - Old devices can be refurbished and reused *[1 mark]* and their raw materials can be recycled. *[1 mark]*

  [2 marks available in total]

3 a) Any **two** ways, e.g.
- Users sometimes leave devices idle / on standby. *[1 mark]*
- Many devices are inefficient (either by design or through lack of servicing) meaning they generate excessive heat, which requires energy to remove through air conditioning. *[1 mark]*
- Users sometimes leave their devices on charge longer than they need to. *[1 mark]*
- Many devices, like servers, very rarely run at their full capacity. This means they are using lots of energy but not doing much with it, so the energy is wasted. *[1 mark]*

[2 marks available in total]

b) E.g.
- Manufacturers can include sleep or hibernation modes in new devices *[1 mark]* to reduce their energy consumption when they are idle. *[1 mark]*
- Manufacturers can design devices to be more energy efficient, *[1 mark]* for example to minimise the amount of heat they generate. *[1 mark]*

[2 marks available in total]

c) E.g.
- Most energy comes from non-renewable sources like coal, gas and oil. *[1 mark]* These resources are scarce. *[1 mark]* Extracting these resources / burning these resources in power stations causes pollution. *[1 mark]*
- As developing countries become developed countries, their energy consumption will increase. *[1 mark]*
- The use of energy from non-renewable resources will accelerate climate change. *[1 mark]*
- The world will need to get more of its energy from renewable sources (like solar, wind and wave) if it is to fulfil the worldwide demand for energy in the future. *[1 mark]*
- More nuclear power stations may need to be built, to which many people are opposed. *[1 mark]*

[4 marks available in total]

This last Q part isn't about how computers use electricity. It's about the bigger picture of how to meet the increasing worldwide demand for energy.

4 Points you might include:

Energy
- The new monitor would be more energy efficient, so there would be less waste of electricity.
- A more energy efficient monitor would mean less electricity would need to be produced for it, which means less pollution.
- The energy saved by using a more energy efficient model may not be enough to make up for the energy used in the creation of the new monitor, which defeats the point of buying an energy efficient monitor.

E-waste
- Throwing away the current monitor would create more e-waste, which could end up in a landfill site. Toxic chemicals in the monitor could leak, causing harm to wildlife and the environment.
- Shaun could look to recycle parts of the monitor or give it to somebody else so they can reuse it.
- It is not clear whether Shaun will keep the new monitor for any longer than his previous monitor. His new monitor could break or he could decide to replace it with yet another monitor.

Natural resources
- The new monitor will use raw materials, which adds to the depletion of natural resources.
- The extraction of raw materials requires more energy, which causes more pollution.

How to mark your answer:
- Two or three brief points with very little explanation. *[1-2 marks]*
- Three to five detailed points covering at least two of: energy, e-waste and natural resources. *[3-5 marks]*
- Six or more detailed points that form a well-written, balanced discussion, covering all of: energy, e-waste and natural resources. *[6-8 marks]*

Pages 44-45: Computer Legislation

Warm-up
- A hospital holds the medical records of its patients so they can be treated — Data Protection Act 2018
- A criminal hacks into a broadband company's network and steals its customers' account details — Computer Misuse Act 1990
- A company is found to be using unlicensed software on all of their computers — Copyright, Designs and Patents Act 1988
- A polling company holds data on members of the public for a survey it is conducting — Data Protection Act 2018
- An employee accesses their manager's network account and deletes company data — Computer Misuse Act 1990

1 a) A data subject is someone whose personal data is stored on somebody else's computer system. *[1 mark]*

b) Any **three** principles, e.g.
- Data must only be used in a fair, lawful and transparent way. *[1 mark]*
- Data must only be used for the specified purpose. *[1 mark]*
- Data should be adequate, relevant and not excessive for the specified use. *[1 mark]*
- Data should not be kept longer than is necessary. *[1 mark]*
- Data should be kept safe and secure. *[1 mark]*

[3 marks available in total]

c) i) E.g. Felix has the right to see, amend and delete any data that the organisation has about him. *[1 mark]*

ii) E.g. An organisation doesn't have to disclose data if it could affect national security / the outcome of a court case. *[1 mark]*

2 a) The legal right that gives the creator of content (e.g. books, music, films, software, video games, etc.) protection over how their content is used. *[1 mark]*

b) Hayley needs to contact the owner of the image *[1 mark]* and request permission to use it. *[1 mark]* Hayley will have to follow the copyright holder's request / acknowledge the source of the image / may have to pay a fee. *[1 mark]*

3 Points you might include:
- The cinema should ask permission from the customer before storing their data.
- The cinema should ask the customer to sign an agreement as to how the information should be used.
- The cinema should only use the data to make it easier for customers to book seats and for contacting them for details on future films.
- The cinema should give customers the option to unsubscribe from their service, so that their data is removed from the cinema's computer system if they want.
- The cinema should be active in keeping its data up to date and allow their customers to change their details.
- The cinema should not give customers' data to third party organisations unless the customer permits it.
- The cinema should ensure that customers' data is held safely and securely, e.g. by using a firewall on its computer system and encrypting the data.

How to mark your answer:
- Two or three brief points with very little explanation. *[1-2 marks]*
- Three or four detailed points that show a good understanding of the Data Protection Act. *[3-4 marks]*
- Five or more detailed points that show a good understanding of the Data Protection Act and clearly apply it to the situation. *[5-6 marks]*

Think about each principle of the Data Protection Act and apply it to this situation.

Answers

Page 46: Open Source and Proprietary Software

Warm-up

Mozilla® Firefox®, Android™, Linux and VLC are open source. Microsoft® PowerPoint®, Adobe® Photoshop® and Microsoft® Word are proprietary.

1 a) Proprietary software is software where only the compiled code is released. *[1 mark]* Users are not allowed to modify, copy or redistribute the software. *[1 mark]*

   b) Any **two** advantages of using proprietary software, e.g.
   - Comes with a warranty / customer support. *[1 mark]*
   - Should be well-tested and reliable. *[1 mark]*
   - Often very secure. *[1 mark]*

   Any **two** disadvantages of using proprietary software, e.g.
   - They may be paying for features they don't need. *[1 mark]*
   - The software may not exactly match their needs and it cannot be modified. *[1 mark]*
   - The software may not gain any new features through updates, as software companies will want to add it to their latest software as a selling point. *[1 mark]*

   [4 marks available in total]

2 a) E.g.
   - Open source software is software where the source code is made freely available. *[1 mark]*
   - Users can legally modify the source code to make their own version of the software. *[1 mark]*
   - Modified versions of the original source code can be shared under the same license as the original software. *[1 mark]*

   [2 marks available in total]

   b) Any **one** advantage and **one** disadvantage, e.g.

   Advantages:
   - It's usually free of charge. *[1 mark]* Free software can be used as a marketing tool — once the device is paid for, the user won't need to pay for any more software. *[1 mark]*
   - The software's source code can be adapted by users *[1 mark]* which may increase the functions of the TV-PC. *[1 mark]*
   - Popular open source software can be very reliable as problems may be quickly fixed by the community or developers *[1 mark]* meaning WeynTeck may not need to work on / push out their own updates. *[1 mark]*

   Disadvantages:
   - They may have unpatched holes in security *[1 mark]*, which could worry customers and reduce sales of the product. *[1 mark]*
   - If there are problems with the open source software *[1 mark]* WeynTeck may not have any support from the software developers. *[1 mark]*
   - WeynTeck won't be able to make money by selling their own proprietary software, *[1 mark]* so they may make less profit from the product overall. *[1 mark]*

   [4 marks available in total]

Pages 47-48: Mixed Questions

1 Points you might include:

   Car and lorry drivers
   - They may receive benefits from having better, faster and shorter journeys.
   - They may see an increase in traffic as the same routes are being used by other car and lorry drivers.

   Technology
   - Widespread use of satellite navigation devices will encourage the development of improvements, e.g. better options to customise routes, easier user interfaces, full speech recognition and wireless charging.
   - Standalone satellite navigation devices could become obsolete as more people use GPS and mapping applications on smartphones.

   Ethical issues
   - Potential for increased risk of accidents as devices are a distraction from driving, although may be better than printed maps.
   - Speed camera detection could encourage reckless driving as drivers can be safe in the knowledge they will be able to foresee speed cameras.

   Environmental issues
   - Widespread use of satellite navigation systems could result in shorter journey times, which means less overall fuel use and less pollution.
   - Satellite navigation devices require disposal when they break, and are less easy to recycle than paper maps.
   - Satellite navigation devices require electricity, which may come from non-renewable sources which cause pollution.
   - Satellite navigation devices may encourage people to make longer journeys by car rather than relying on public transport which could increase pollution.

   How to mark your answer:
   - Two or three brief points with very little explanation. *[1-2 marks]*
   - Three to five detailed points covering at least two of: car and lorry drivers, technology, ethical issues and environmental issues *[3-5 marks]*
   - Six or more detailed points that form a well-written, balanced discussion, covering all of: car and lorry drivers, technology, ethical issues and environmental issues. *[6-8 marks]*

2 Points you might include:

   Technology
   - The need to be able to contact anyone at any time on social media may increase the demand for smartphones and other mobile / wearable devices.
   - Software has adapted to suit social media needs. Many apps include 'share over social media' options. New social media apps and websites have been created in the hope of giving users (and advertisers) a new social media experience (e.g. Snapchat).

   Ethical issues
   - Social media increases the potential for cyberbullying and trolling, which could cause distress among its users.
   - Social media increases the potential for stalking and spying on others.
   - The significant time spent on social media means face-to-face interaction can be ignored.
   - The constant feedback and mental simulation gained from social media can be addictive for some people.

   Privacy issues
   - Social media encourages users to expand their online network of friends so that the social media company can gain new users and therefore more advertising revenue. This could affect people's privacy as they can share personal information with people they barely know.
   - Social media tends to have lax security settings by default. This means the information people share on social media can often be viewed by those for which it was not intended.

Answers

Cultural issues

- Social media allows people with a range of different identities, opinions and backgrounds to communicate and share information with others. This allows people who don't normally get a voice to be heard, and allows other social media users to be exposed to a diverse range of views and experiences.
- Social media allows people with specific interests to more easily support causes they care about and meet like-minded people.
- Social media encourages users to post their views and photographs (including 'selfies') which contributes to a culture which might be becoming more self-centred and vain.

How to mark your answer:
- Two or three brief points with very little explanation. *[1-2 marks]*
- Three to five detailed points covering at least two of: technology, ethical issues, privacy issues and cultural issues. *[3-5 marks]*
- Six or more detailed points that form a well-written, balanced discussion, covering all of: technology, ethical issues, privacy issues and cultural issues. *[6-8 marks]*

3 Points you might include:

Customers and shop owners

- Shop owners will have to invest in new technology to allow payment from phones.
- Customers will always have a way of paying even if they forget their wallet.

Technology

- Mobile phones need to be designed with the appropriate hardware and software to make use of payment systems.
- Mobile phones need to have high quality security software to prevent theft and fraud.
- Mobile phones need to have a long battery life to ensure that people are not stranded without a way to make purchases.
- Mobile phone developers need to work with shops, banks and other retailers to make sure they have the technology to accept payments from mobile phones.

Ethical issues

- Transactions are easier on digital payment systems and the money is never visible. This may encourage people to spend more money, increasing the likelihood of them getting into debt.
- Digital payment may encourage more widespread hacking and computer misuse.

Environmental issues

- There is no need to dispose of old notes and coins, although e-waste caused by broken mobile devices arguably causes greater environmental damage.
- If digital payment systems become more popular, physical coins and notes may no longer be required and need to be disposed of.

How to mark your answer:
- Two or three brief points with very little explanation. *[1-2 marks]*
- Three to five detailed points covering at least two of: customers and shop owners, technology, ethical issues and environmental issues. *[3-5 marks]*
- Six or more detailed points that form a well-written, balanced discussion, covering all of: customers and shop owners, technology, ethical issues and environmental issues. *[6-8 marks]*

4 Points you might include:

Consumers and businesses

- Consumers will be able to access a greater variety of books, films and music. They will be able to purchase them at their own convenience without having to go to a shop. The books, films and music should also be cheaper as the costs are much lower to produce digital copies than physical copies.
- Traditional bookshops, CD shops and film retailers will have to adapt to distributing their stock digitally or face a decline in profits.
- New businesses that distribute books, music and films digitally could flourish as they gain some of the traditional stores' market share. New business models have been founded to distribute digital media, e.g. subscription-based services or streaming services where money is made through advertising.

Technology

- Use of digital media has encouraged the development and improvement in technology. E.g. e-readers introduced a new type of display technology that looks and feels more like a printed book. In the future, displays which are even more paper-like may be used.
- The use of digital media has placed extra demands on communication networks. This creates a cycle of improvement, e.g. watching high-quality films increases demand for better broadband speeds, which in turn encourages people to watch higher quality films, increasing demand for good broadband.
- The use of digital media is changing TVs from devices that receive broadcasted transmissions to Internet-enabled devices used to stream media from the Internet.

Environmental issues

- Less use of physical media means there could be less physical waste from packaging and discarded books, CDs and DVDs.
- No need for packaging or physical media, so fewer natural resources required in the distribution of the media.
- Greater use of digital media means increased use of electricity, as well as increased e-waste if hardware is discarded.

Legal issues

- Use of digital media could increase the amount of illegal file sharing.
- It is often unclear who owns the copyright to the original piece of work, and how profit from the book / music / film should be shared. E.g. how much money should a musician receive from their music being listened to on a free streaming service.
- It is often unclear who owns the digital file. E.g. should someone be able to pass their movie files onto their children, or does the ownership over them go back to the original distributor.

How to mark your answer:
- Two or three brief points with very little explanation. *[1-2 marks]*
- Three to five detailed points covering at least two of: consumers and businesses, technology, environmental issues and legal issues. *[3-5 marks]*
- Six or more detailed points that form a well-written, balanced discussion, covering all of: consumers and businesses, technology, environmental issues and legal issues. *[6-8 marks]*

Section Five — Algorithms

Page 49: Computational Thinking

Warm-Up

Decomposition is breaking down a complex problem into smaller problems and **solving** each one **individually**.
Abstraction is picking out the **important** bits of **information** from the problem, ignoring the specific **details** that don't matter.

1 a) Any **two** decomposition and matching abstraction processes.
E.g.
- Decomposition: What will the keyboard look like? *[1 mark]*
Abstraction: Ignore the colour and material. Focus on the layout and size. *[1 mark]*
- Decomposition: Which computers should it be compatible with? *[1 mark]*
Abstraction: Ignore computers and operating systems more than 10 years old. Focus on newest and most common computers and operating systems. *[1 mark]*
- Decomposition: Are there any competitor keyboards? *[1 mark]*
Abstraction: Ignore make and model names. Focus on price, features and quality. *[1 mark]*
[4 marks available in total]

b) Using logical steps to find a solution to a complex problem. *[1 mark]*

2 a) E.g. Abstraction is picking out important details and ignoring irrelevant ones. The file uploading service will focus on the important details like the file name and ignore the unimportant details like the contents of each file.
[3 marks available — 1 mark for a definition of abstraction, 1 mark for an example of a detail to ignore, 1 mark for an example of a detail to focus on]

b) E.g. Decomposition breaks the programming task down into smaller problems. A programmer might focus on 'How will the service keep track of files already uploaded?' or 'How will the service compare file names?' and try to solve each programming problem individually.
[3 marks available — 1 mark for a definition of decomposition, 1 mark for each example of decomposition up to a maximum of 2 marks]

Pages 50-52: Writing Algorithms

Warm-Up

Input | Stop | Decision | Process

1 a) An algorithm is a process or set of instructions used to solve a problem. *[1 mark]*

b) It asks the user to input a height and width. *[1 mark]*
It then multiplies these values together *[1 mark]*
to get the area and prints the value of the area. *[1 mark]*

c) 5 × 10 = 50 *[1 mark]*

2 Asking for user input. *[1 mark]*
Comparing parcel number with requirement of eight characters. *[1 mark]*
Outputting "Valid parcel number." for correct cases. *[1 mark]*
Outputting "Not a valid parcel number." for invalid cases. *[1 mark]*
E.g.
input parcelNumber
if parcelNumber has 8 characters then
    output "Valid parcel number"
else
    output "Not a valid parcel number"
endif

3 a) Any **one** problem, e.g.
- No Start / Begin box. *[1 mark]*
- No Stop / End box. *[1 mark]*
[1 mark available in total]

b) 10 × 8 ÷ 5 = 16 km *[1 mark]*

c) Using Start / Begin. *[1 mark]*
8/5 changed to 1.6093. *[1 mark]*
Decision box with appropriate question. *[1 mark]*
Creating a loop to input a new distance. *[1 mark]*
Using Stop / End. *[1 mark]*
E.g.

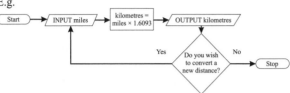

4 a) Decision box with appropriate question. *[1 mark]*
Output for winning ticket. *[1 mark]*
Output for losing ticket. *[1 mark]*
Using Stop / End. *[1 mark]*
E.g.

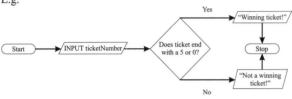

b) Using Start / Begin. *[1 mark]*
Using a counter to track number of tickets. *[1 mark]*
Using ticket sub program appropriately. *[1 mark]*
Creating a loop that repeats 10 times. *[1 mark]*
Decision box with appropriate question. *[1 mark]*
Using Stop / End. *[1 mark]*
E.g.

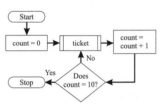

5 Using Start / Begin. *[1 mark]*
Asking user to input *x*, *y*. *[1 mark]*
Using SqMove (with correct sub program box). *[1 mark]*
Decision box with appropriate question. *[1 mark]*
Creating a loop to repeat SqMove. *[1 mark]*
Using Stop / End. *[1 mark]*
E.g.

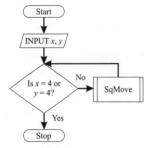

Answers

6 a) Using Start / Begin. *[1 mark]*
Decision boxes with appropriate questions. *[1 mark]*
Calculate discounts for existing customers correctly. *[1 mark]*
Calculate £5 off for costs ≥ £50 (new customers). *[1 mark]*
Arrows and Yes / No labels correctly drawn. *[1 mark]*
Using Stop / End. *[1 mark]*
E.g.

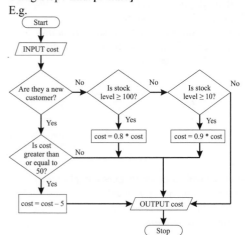

You could also use a decision box with three outcomes to check for each of the three possible stock levels.

b) Follow your flowchart to find the cost, e.g.

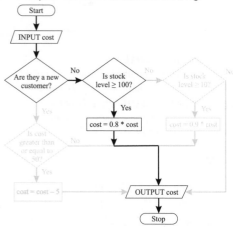

0.8 × £100 = £80 *[1 mark]*

Page 53: Search Algorithms

1 a) A binary search only works on ordered data. *[1 mark]*

b) Check the first item: 2 ≠ 13.
Check the second item: 3 ≠ 13.
Check the third item: 7 ≠ 13.
Check the fourth item: 5 ≠ 13.
Check the fifth item: 13 = 13.
Stop searching as the item has be found.
[2 marks available — 1 mark for starting with 2, 1 mark for checking items in order until you find 13]

2 a) Compare butterscotch to mint. *[1 mark]*
Mint is greater so split and take the left side. *[1 mark]*
A further comparison. *[1 mark]*
Correct identification of butterscotch. *[1 mark]*
E.g.
Middle item = (5 + 1) / 2 = 3rd item = mint.
Compare mint with butterscotch.
Butterscotch comes before mint, so take left hand side.
The list is: Butterscotch, Chocolate.
Middle item = (2 + 1) / 2 = 1.5 = 2nd item = chocolate.
Compare chocolate to butterscotch.
Butterscotch comes before chocolate, so take left hand side.
Middle item = (1 + 1) / 2 = 1st item = butterscotch.
Stop searching as butterscotch has been found.

b) It is much more efficient / takes fewer steps for large lists of items. *[1 mark]*
You won't get the mark for just saying it's quicker or more efficient.

c) There will be 11 items in total — so the middle item will be the (11 + 1) / 2 = 6th item. *[1 mark]*
The 9th item is after the 6th so take the right side. *[1 mark]*
This reduced list includes the 7th to 11th items of the original list — so 5 items in total.
Check the middle item which will the (5 + 1) / 2 = 3rd item of the reduced list (which is the 9th item of the original list).
It has taken 2 iterations to find the 9th item. *[1 mark]*

Pages 54-55: Sorting Algorithms

1

Riga	**Paris**	Oslo	Baku	Minsk
Paris	Riga	**Oslo**	Baku	Minsk
Oslo	Paris	Riga	**Baku**	Minsk
Baku	Oslo	Paris	Riga	**Minsk**
Baku	Minsk	Oslo	Paris	Riga

[4 marks available — 1 mark for each row from rows 2-5]

2 1st pass: 5 comparisons, 3 swaps.

5.32 m	**5.50 m**	5.39 m	6.50 m	6.28 m	6.14 m
5.32 m	**5.39 m**	**5.50 m**	6.50 m	6.28 m	6.14 m
5.32 m	5.39 m	**5.50 m**	**6.50 m**	6.28 m	6.14 m
5.32 m	5.39 m	5.50 m	**6.28 m**	**6.50 m**	6.14 m
5.32 m	5.39 m	5.50 m	6.28 m	**6.14 m**	**6.50 m**

2nd pass: 4 comparisons, 1 swap.

5.32 m	**5.39 m**	5.50 m	6.28 m	6.14 m	6.50 m
5.32 m	**5.39 m**	**5.50 m**	6.28 m	6.14 m	6.50 m
5.32 m	5.39 m	**5.50 m**	**6.28 m**	6.14 m	6.50 m
5.32 m	5.39 m	5.50 m	**6.14 m**	**6.28 m**	6.50 m

3rd pass: 3 comparisons, no swaps, list is ordered.

5.32 m	5.39 m	5.50 m	6.14 m	6.28 m	6.50 m

You can do multiple swaps in one stage but make it clear in your bubble sort if you do this.
[4 marks available — 1 mark for each correct swap]

3 a) i)

3	**7**	6	2	5
7	3	**6**	2	5
7	6	3	**2**	5
7	6	3	2	**5**
7	6	5	3	2

[4 marks available — 1 mark for each row from rows 2-5]

ii) E.g.

3 | 7 | 6 | 2 | 5

3 7   6 2 5

3   7   6   2 5

3   7   6   2   5

7 3   6   5 2

7 3   6 5 2

7 6 5 3 2

[4 marks available — 1 mark for correctly splitting the list into single items, 1 mark for each correct merging row]
The list doesn't split evenly so there is more than one way to get the right answer depending on how you split the items.

b) Any **one** benefit of insertion sort with contrast to merge sort, e.g.
- Insertion sort uses less memory *[1 mark]* as, unlike a merge sort, all the sorting is done on the original list. *[1 mark]*
- Insertion sort is quicker to check if a list is in order *[1 mark]* as a merge sort would still need to go through the splitting–merging process. *[1 mark]*

[2 marks available in total]

4 a)
| 450 | 350 | 230 | 180 | 650 | 500 | 340 | 270 |

| 450 | 350 | 230 | 180 | | 650 | 500 | 340 | 270 |

| 450 | 350 | | 230 | 180 | | 650 | 500 | | 340 | 270 |

| 450 | 350 | 230 | 180 | 650 | 500 | 340 | 270 |

| 350 | 450 | 180 | 230 | 500 | 650 | 270 | 340 |

| 180 | 230 | 350 | 450 | 270 | 340 | 500 | 650 |

| 180 | 230 | 270 | 340 | 350 | 450 | 500 | 650 |

[4 marks available — 1 mark for correctly splitting the list into single items, 1 mark for each correct merging row]

b) i) Small lists are easier to sort than larger lists. *[1 mark]*

   ii) Ordered lists will be easier to merge at the next step of the algorithm. *[1 mark]*

5 a) It compares the first pair of elements in the array and swaps them if the first element is bigger. *[1 mark]* It then repeats for each other pair of elements in the array. *[1 mark]*

b) E.g. The while loop repeats while the *sorted* variable is false. *[1 mark]* *sorted* is set to true at the start of the while loop, but is set back to false if any swaps take place. *[1 mark]* If there are no swaps in a pass (e.g. when the array is sorted) then the *sorted* variable remains true and the algorithm ends. *[1 mark]*

c) Bubble sort *[1 mark]*

Pages 56-57: Mixed Questions

1 a) Any **one** decomposition and matching abstraction process, e.g.
- Decomposition: Where is the tour? *[1 mark]*
  Abstraction: Ignore full venue address.
  Focus on the venue name and the city. *[1 mark]*
- What names should go on the advert? *[1 mark]*
  Ignore band members' names. Focus on the name of the band (and supporting bands). *[1 mark]*
- Where can tickets be bought? *[1 mark]*
  Ignore local retailers. Focus on ticket websites. *[1 mark]*

[2 marks available in total]

b) It would cost a basic user £5 + £1 = £6 and a premium user 5 × 0.5 = £2.50. *[1 mark]*
The difference is £6 – £2.50 = £3.50. *[1 mark]*

2 a) Check each item in order.
Check the first item: 10 mA ≠ 12 mA
Check the second item: 15 mA ≠ 12 mA
Check the third item: 12 mA = 12 mA.
Stop searching as the item has been found.
[2 marks available — 1 mark for starting with 10 mA, 1 mark for checking items in order until you find 12 mA]

b) Using Start / Begin. *[1 mark]*
Input to check reading. *[1 mark]*
Decision box with appropriate question. *[1 mark]*
'Buzz' as an output. *[1 mark]*
Wait 5 minutes as a process. *[1 mark]*
Using Stop / End. *[1 mark]*
E.g.

3 a) *Use abbreviations to reduce the size of the algorithm:*

| Fl | Po | Ri | Va | Pa | Hi |

| Fl | Po | Ri | | Va | Pa | Hi |

| Fl | Po | Ri | | Va | | Pa | Hi |

| Fl | Po | Ri | Va | | Pa | Hi |

| Fl | Po | Ri | Va | Hi | Pa |

| Fl | Po | Ri | Hi | Pa | Va |

| Fl | Hi | Pa | Po | Ri | Va |

[4 marks available — 1 mark for correctly splitting the list into single items, 1 mark for each correct merging row]
The list doesn't split evenly so there is more than one way to get the right answer depending on how you split the items.

b) Compare Rings to Pommel. *[1 mark]*
Rings is greater so split and take the right side. *[1 mark]*
A further comparison. *[1 mark]*
Correct identification of Rings. *[1 mark]*
E.g.
Middle item = (6 + 1) / 2 = 3.5 = 4th item = Pommel.
Compare Pommel with Rings.
Rings is after Pommel, so take right hand side.
List becomes Rings, Vault
Middle item = (2 + 1) / 2 = 1.5 = 2nd item = Vault.
Rings is before Vault, so take left hand side.
List becomes Rings
Middle item = (1 + 1) / 2 = 1st item = Rings.
Stop searching as Rings has been found.

4 a) Using Start / Begin. *[1 mark]*
Input the outcome of two dice rolls. *[1 mark]*
Decision boxes with appropriate questions. *[1 mark]*
Calculating the score correctly and outputting it. *[1 mark]*
Arrows and Yes / No labels correctly drawn. *[1 mark]*
Using Stop / End. *[1 mark]*
E.g.

b) Linear Search *[1 mark]* — the list is unlikely to be ordered, so you couldn't use a binary search. *[1 mark]*

Section Six — Programming

Pages 58-59: Programming Basics

Warm-up

The number of people on a football pitch.
The age of a pet in whole months.
The number on a rolled dice.
The length of a car to the nearest metre.

1   Flavour — String *[1 mark]*
    Weight (kg) — Real / Float *[1 mark]*
    Quantity in stock — Integer *[1 mark]*
    Gluten-Free? — Boolean *[1 mark]*

2   a)   Takes the string "76423" and returns the integer 76423.
      [1 mark]

    b)   Returns the ASCII number for the character 'T'. *[1 mark]*

    c)   Returns the remainder when 12 is divided by 5, i.e. 2 *[1 mark]*

3   Boolean *[1 mark]* — the variable can only take two values,
   either pressed or not pressed, i.e. true or false. *[1 mark]*

4   a)   z = x + y *[1 mark]*

    b)   z = x >= y *[1 mark]*

    c)   z = (x + y) / 160 * 100 *[1 mark]*

5   a)   i)   String *[1 mark]*

       ii)   Real / Float *[1 mark]*

    b)   Using the correct data type will make your programs more
      memory efficient. *[1 mark]* It will also make your programs
      more robust and predictable. *[1 mark]*

    c)   E.g. All the different data values might be converted to strings
      using the str() function so string concatenation can be used to
      join them together on the receipt. *[1 mark]* For example the
      cost of fuel might be converted from a real / float to a string
      so it can be printed in a sentence, e.g. "The cost of fuel was
      £20.76". *[1 mark]*

Page 60: Constants and Variables

1   a)   toppings *[1 mark]*
      eatIn *[1 mark]*

    b)   £1 *[1 mark]*

    c)   Any **two** reasons, e.g.
      • It doesn't need to be changed as the program is running.
        [1 mark]
      • Updating the value of a constant once will update it
        everywhere in the program. *[1 mark]*
      • It'll produce more meaningful code — a constant name of
        toppingsCost is clearer than 0.5. *[1 mark]*
      [2 marks available in total]

2   Investment is declared as a constant but its value changes. *[1 mark]*
   Rate has a string type but should have a real/float type. *[1 mark]*

3   E.g.
   Constant: An integer constant for the maximum number of
   customers allowed in the gym *[1 mark]* because it will never need
   to change. *[1 mark]*
   Variable 1: An integer variable for the current number of customers
   in the gym *[1 mark]* as the value will need to change whenever
   someone enters or leaves the gym. *[1 mark]*
   Variable 2: A Boolean variable to decide whether a card scan gains
   entry to the gym or not *[1 mark]* as the value will need to update
   every time a card is scanned. *[1 mark]*
   *Any appropriate constant / variable with a valid explanation will gain
   2 marks.*

Page 61: Strings

Warm-up

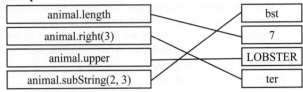

1   a)   14 *[1 mark]*

    b)   82016 *[1 mark]*

    c)   JAN *[1 mark]*

2   a)   Joining together two or more strings. *[1 mark]*

    b)   ORA2000 *[1 mark]*

    c)   03   fruit = fruit.upper *[1 mark]*
      04   prodID = fruit.left(3) *[1 mark]*
          + str(volume) *[1 mark]*
      *You could have used fruit.subString(0, 3)
      instead of fruit.left(3) in line 04.*

Pages 62-64: Program Flow

Warm-up

Selection Statements: IF-THEN-ELSE, SWITCH, IF-ELSEIF
Iteration Statements: DO UNTIL, WHILE

1   a)   Sequence *[1 mark]*

    b)   2 hours and 30 minutes *[1 mark]*

2   Asking for an input from the user. *[1 mark]*
   Condition-controlled loop with appropriate condition. *[1 mark]*
   Appropriate feedback for a valid password. *[1 mark]*
   E.g.
   do
     password = input("Please enter a password")
   until password.length >=6
   print("Your password is valid")
   *Your answer must use the correct syntax if you've used a
   high-level programming language for your answer.*

3   a)   Using a SWITCH statement. *[1 mark]*
      Using correct cases for all settings. *[1 mark]*
      Changing the temperature correctly for each setting. *[1 mark]*
      E.g.
      setting = input()
      switch setting:
        case "3":
          temperature = 50
        case "2":
          temperature = 30
        case "1":
          temperature = 20
        default:
          temperature = 0
      endswitch

    b)   Any **two** reasons, e.g.
      • You only need to check the value of one variable. *[1 mark]*
      • The setting variable only has a set number of possible values.
        [1 mark]

4   a)   Boolean *[1 mark]*

    b)   The player always gets the same number of shots *[1 mark]*
      so you don't need to check a condition, just repeat the loop
      10 times. *[1 mark]*

    c)   The FOR loop will repeat more times,
      giving the player more shots. *[1 mark]*

    d)   The game should check after every shot if the score is equal to
      5. *[1 mark]* A condition-controlled loop will keep repeating
      the game until the player has scored 5. *[1 mark]*

5   Using a condition controlled loop. *[1 mark]*
Waiting for an input from user for keypress. *[1 mark]*
Concatenating keypress with the sentence. *[1 mark]*
Using the correct terminating condition. *[1 mark]*
Printing the sentence. *[1 mark]*
E.g.
sentence = " "
do
   keypress = input()
   sentence = sentence + keypress
until keypress == "." OR keypress == "?" OR keypress == "!"
print(sentence)

6   Count controlled loop to allow 10 games. *[1 mark]*
Asking for an input of the winner's name for each game. *[1 mark]*
A selection statement for the winner of each game. *[1 mark]*
Adding 1 to the winner's score. *[1 mark]*
A selection statement to find the overall winner. *[1 mark]*
Printing the correct message depending on the scores. *[1 mark]*
E.g.
karlWin = 0
johnWin = 0
for i = 1 to 10
   winner = input("Enter the winner's name.")
   if winner == "Karl" then
      karlWin = karlWin + 1
   elseif winner == "John" then
      johnWin = johnWin + 1
   endif
next i
if karlWin > johnWin then
   print("The winner is Karl.")
elseif johnWin > karlWin then
   print("The winner is John.")
else
   print("The game is a draw.")
endif
To make your algorithm more robust you could have used input validation to make sure winner was either "Karl" or "John". You could also have named the variables differently so that the game could be played by any two players regardless of their name.

Pages 65-67: Boolean Logic

Warm-up

12 > 4 AND 5 == 5
12 <= 4 OR 10 != 5
NOT(11 == 3)
NOT(9 > 4 AND 5 < 2)

1   a)

[1 mark]

  b)

[1 mark]

2   a)   B = 0 *[1 mark]*

  b)   A = 1, B = 1 *[1 mark]*
A and B must both be 1 for the output of an AND gate to be 1. The NOT gate changes the 1 to a 0.

3   a)   "Warning — Please alter the temperature." *[1 mark]*

  b)   "Warning — Please alter the humidity." *[1 mark]*

4   a)

A	B	Q
FALSE	FALSE	TRUE
FALSE	TRUE	FALSE
TRUE	FALSE	TRUE
TRUE	TRUE	TRUE

[3 marks available — 1 mark for each correct row]

  b)   The NOT logic gate is pointing the wrong way. *[1 mark]*
The OR gate should only have one output. *[1 mark]*

5   a)

[3 marks available — 1 mark for inputs S and D going into an AND gate, 1 mark for the output of AND gate and input I going into an OR gate, 1 mark for Z being the OR gate output]

  b)   (S AND D) OR I = Z *[1 mark]*

  c)   i)   S = 0, D = 1, I = 0, Z = 0 *[1 mark]*
      ii)   S = 1, D = 1, I = 1, Z = 1 *[1 mark]*
         S = 1, D = 0, I = 1, Z = 1 *[1 mark]*

6   a)

A	B	C	NOT A	B AND C	(NOT A) AND (B AND C)
0	0	0	1	0	0
0	0	1	1	0	0
0	1	0	1	0	0
0	1	1	1	1	1
1	0	0	0	0	0
1	0	1	0	0	0
1	1	0	0	0	0
1	1	1	0	1	0

[3 marks available — 1 mark for each correct column]

  b)

[3 marks available — 1 mark for input A going into a NOT gate, 1 mark for inputs B and C going into an AND gate, 1 mark for outputs going into an AND gate with one output]

7   Using an appropriate selection statement. *[1 mark]*
A Boolean condition to check if the driver has paid or has a permit. *[1 mark]*
Appropriate barrier conditions. *[1 mark]*
E.g.
Insert a ticket or permit
if ticketPaid == true OR permitValid == true then
   barrierUp = true
else
   barrierUp = false
endif

8   Using an appropriate selection statement. *[1 mark]*
A Boolean condition that checks each of the conditions. *[1 mark]*
Allowing the dryer to start if conditions are met. *[1 mark]*
E.g.
Check weight and door
if (weight > 1.5 AND weight < 15.0) AND doorClosed == true then
   allowStart = true
else
   allowStart = false
endif

Page 68: Random Number Generation

Warm-up

3, 4, 5, 6, 7 and 8

1   Generating a random integer from 0 to 4 *[1 mark]*
Using this to choose a tea from the array *[1 mark]*
Outputting a suitable message using the chosen tea *[1 mark]*
E.g.
randNum = random(0, 4)
chosenTea = teaTypes[randNum]
print("This morning, have a " + chosenTea + " tea.")

2 a) Any **two** reasons, e.g.
- So that the game is different each time it is played. *[1 mark]*
- To simulate something that is random in real life, e.g. weather, dice rolls, etc. *[1 mark]*
- So that the game is unpredictable and challenging. *[1 mark]*
- So that the developer can let the game generate things like characters or environments, rather than creating them manually. *[1 mark]*

  [2 marks available in total]

b) E.g. The random function could produce the same number more than once, which would produce the same card twice. *[1 mark]* This is not intended, as when a card is drawn it should be removed from the deck. *[1 mark]*

Pages 69-70: Arrays

1 a) 440 500 *[1 mark]*

b) 510 000 – 429 000 = 81 000 *[1 mark]*

c) if highscores[4] < newScore then
     Update the array.
   endif
   [2 marks available — 1 mark for using the element in position 4 of the array, 1 mark for checking if the newScore is greater than that element]

2 a) Declaring a three element array. *[1 mark]*
   Correctly asking for the user input. *[1 mark]*
   Correctly assigning the inputs to the array. *[1 mark]*
   E.g.
   array cupcakes[3]
   cupcakes[0] = input("Enter first flavour")
   cupcakes[1] = input("Enter second flavour")
   cupcakes[2] = input("Enter third flavour")
   You could also use a FOR loop for this question.

b) *print(cupcakes[1]) [1 mark]*

c) E.g. replace the second line of code with:
   cupcakes[0] = "Raspberry" [1 mark]

3 a) String *[1 mark]*

b) Any **three** reasons, e.g.
- Multiple items of data need to be stored. *[1 mark]*
- All the data being stored has the same data type. *[1 mark]*
- The data is split by two categories / can be represented in a table so a 2D array is useful for storing it. *[1 mark]*
- Stores the data together under one variable name. *[1 mark]*
- Accessing the information is more efficient. A single command, e.g. *sportsDay[position, event]* can be used to access any name from the array. *[1 mark]*

  [3 marks available in total — at least one reason must specifically mention 2D arrays.]

4 a) print(distanceRun[4, 3]) *[1 mark]*

b) Asking the user to input the runner number. *[1 mark]*
   Using a FOR loop. *[1 mark]*
   Adding all elements correctly. *[1 mark]*
   Printing the total distance. *[1 mark]*
   E.g.
   totalDistance = 0
   runner = input("Choose a runner number from 0-3")
   for i = 0 to 6
   * totalDistance = totalDistance + distanceRun[i, runner]*
   next i
   print(totalDistance)

c) A FOR loop going from 0 to 3. *[1 mark]*
   A FOR loop going from 0 to 6. *[1 mark]*
   Using milesConvert() on each element of the array. *[1 mark]*
   E.g.
   for i = 0 to 3
   * for j = 0 to 6*
   *   distanceRun[i, j] = milesConvert(distanceRun[i, j])*
   * next j*
   next i

Page 71: File Handling

1 a) Line 01: Opens the file and assigns it to a variable called myList. *[1 mark]*
   Line 02: Prints the first line of the file: "1. Clean my room." *[1 mark]*
   Line 03: Closes the file *[1 mark]*

b) The writeLine command will start writing from the end of the file *[1 mark]* so the new line of text will be added to the end of the text file instead of overwriting the first line. *[1 mark]*

2 Opening the story. *[1 mark]*
   A condition-controlled loop to stop at the end of the file. *[1 mark]*
   Waiting for a keypress input. *[1 mark]*
   Using a selection statement to check the user's input. *[1 mark]*
   Printing the next line of the story. *[1 mark]*
   E.g.
   story = open("adventure.txt")
   while NOT story.endOfFile()
   * keypress = input()*
   * if keypress == "y" then*
   *   print(story.readLine())*
   * endif*
   endwhile
   story.close()

Pages 72-73: Storing and Searching Data

1 Text / String *[1 mark]*
  Integer *[1 mark]*
  Real / Float *[1 mark]*
  Text / String *[1 mark]*
  Boolean *[1 mark]*

2 a) 5 *[1 mark]*

b) A record is a data structure used to store multiple pieces of data about one thing together (e.g. information about a particular car). *[1 mark]* A field is one of the items in a record that contains a particular piece of data (e.g. car registration or car make). *[1 mark]*
   Just saying that records are rows of the table and fields are columns will not be awarded any marks.

c) i)

Registration	Make
FQ55 ALW	Stanton
SQ57 TTW	Fenwick

   [2 marks available — 1 mark for each correct record]

   ii)

Make	Type
Fenwick	Saloon
Stanton	Saloon

   [2 marks available — 1 mark for each correct record]

3 a) String *[1 mark]*

b) Any **two** reasons, e.g.
- Records separate data about different pupils. *[1 mark]*
- Records keep all data about a specific pupil together. *[1 mark]*
- Records make retrieving data about pupils easier. *[1 mark]*

  [2 marks available in total]

c) It will return all the records that are Year 10 pupils *[1 mark]* and it will show every field. *[1 mark]*

4 a) E.g. Storing the data in records allows the different fields to have different data types *[1 mark]* while if they used an array, they would all have to be the same data type. *[1 mark]*

b) i) SELECT Rating FROM comics
WHERE Title = "Hike of Hope"
[2 marks available — 1 mark for selecting the correct fields from the comics table, 1 mark for a correct 'where' statement]

ii) SELECT Title FROM comics
WHERE Genre = "Science Fiction"
[2 marks available — 1 mark for selecting the correct fields from the comics table, 1 mark for a correct 'where' statement]

iii) SELECT Title, Length FROM comics
WHERE Length < 50
[2 marks available — 1 mark for selecting the correct fields from the comics table, 1 mark for a correct 'where' statement]

Pages 74-75: Sub Programs

1 A function that takes a single parameter. *[1 mark]*
Finding the cube and square of the integer. *[1 mark]*
Returning the difference between the cube and square. *[1 mark]*
E.g.

```
function cubeSquare(num)
    return(num^3 – num^2)
endfunction
```

2 a) Any **three** benefits, e.g.
- She will only have to write them once so she doesn't have to repeat blocks of code. *[1 mark]*
- She can call them from anywhere in the program. *[1 mark]*
- She only has to debug them once. *[1 mark]*
- They will improve the readability / maintainability of her code. *[1 mark]*
- They break the program down into smaller more manageable chunks. *[1 mark]*
[3 marks available in total]

b) A function will return a value, a procedure will not. *[1 mark]*

3 a) Any **two** reasons, e.g.
- Local variables can only be changed and accessed from within the sub program they're declared in. *[1 mark]* This prevents programmers from accidentally affecting things in different parts of a program. *[1 mark]*
- A local variable 'disappears' outside of the sub program, *[1 mark]* which means that you could declare the same variable name twice without it creating a conflict. *[1 mark]*
- A sub program with only local variables is self-contained *[1 mark]* so you could reuse it in a different program without having to declare any variables beforehand. *[1 mark]*
[4 marks available in total]

b) A function that takes the number of sides the dice have as a parameter. *[1 mark]*
Using a condition controlled loop. *[1 mark]*
Using the rollTwo function. *[1 mark]*
Increasing the score by 1 after each roll. *[1 mark]*
Returning the score. *[1 mark]*
E.g.

```
function rollGame(sides)
    score = 0
    do
        results = rollTwo(sides)
        score = score + 1
    until results[0] == results[1]
    return score
endfunction
```

4 a) i) A parameter is a special variable that passes data into a sub program. *[1 mark]*

ii) Parameters have a local scope to the sub program they're defined in. *[1 mark]*

b) i) Declares a new variable, difficulty, and assigns it a value of 0 *[1 mark]*. The variable has global scope so it can be used anywhere in the program. *[1 mark]*

ii) It takes weight as a parameter *[1 mark]* and sets the variable difficulty equal to the integer (quotient) part when weight is divided by 6. *[1 mark]*

c) A sub program that takes heart rate as a parameter. *[1 mark]*
Using a selection statement. *[1 mark]*
Having correct conditions on the selection statement. *[1 mark]*
Setting the difficulty depending on the conditions. *[1 mark]*
E.g.

```
procedure adjustLevel(heartrate)
    if heartrate > 160 then
        difficulty = 0
        print("Slow Down!")
    elseif heartrate < 90 then
        difficulty = difficulty + 1
    elseif heartrate > 140 then
        difficulty = difficulty – 1
    endif
endprocedure
```

Pages 76-77: Mixed Questions

1 a) String *[1 mark]*
Integer *[1 mark]*

b) Using a selection statement. *[1 mark]*
Using the correct conditions. *[1 mark]*
Altering the power depending on the condition. *[1 mark]*
Printing the setting and power correctly. *[1 mark]*
Printing an error if an invalid setting is used. *[1 mark]*
E.g.

```
setting = input("Choose setting.")
switch setting:
    case "Defrost":
        power = 200
    case "Medium":
        power = 650
    case "High":
        power = 900
    default:
        print("Error - invalid setting")
endswitch
print(setting + " " + str(power) + "W")
```

2 a) 55.0 *[1 mark]*
The output should be a real / float.

b) Declaring a procedure that takes the new average speed as a parameter. *[1 mark]*
Using an appropriate iteration statement. *[1 mark]*
Moving the elements in the array to the next position. *[1 mark]*
Updating position 0 of the array with the new average speed. *[1 mark]*
E.g.

```
procedure updateSpeeds(newSpeed)
    for i = 9 to 1
        journeySpeeds[i] = journeySpeeds[i-1]
    next i
    journeySpeeds[0] = newSpeed
endprocedure
```

Hint: Remember that the last element of the array is in position 9, not position 10.

3 a) array primeKoalas[4, 2]
primeKoalas[0, 0] = "John"
primeKoalas[1, 0] = "Paul"
primeKoalas[2, 0] = "Cheryl"
primeKoalas[3, 0] = "Ida"
primeKoalas[0, 1] = "guitar"
primeKoalas[1, 1] = "bass"
primeKoalas[2, 1] = "vocals"
primeKoalas[3, 1] = "drums"
[2 marks available — 2 marks for all 4 correct lines of code, otherwise 1 mark for at least two correct lines of code]

b) Creating a new text file named "musicians.txt". *[1 mark]*
Opening and closing the file properly. *[1 mark]*
Using a loop. *[1 mark]*
Writing the name and instrument of each band member to the file. *[1 mark]*
E.g.
newFile("musicians.txt")
band = open("musicians.txt")
for i = 0 to 3
  band.writeLine(primeKoalas[i, 0] + " " + primeKoalas[i, 1])
next i
band.close()

c) Any **two** advantages with explanations, e.g.
- Text files don't lose data when the program stops. *[1 mark]* So the program can pick up where it left off the next time it runs. *[1 mark]*
- Text files can be accessed at any time. *[1 mark]* So data can be read from or written to them even when the program isn't running. *[1 mark]*
- Text files give you more flexibility over what you can store. *[1 mark]* You don't need to worry about data types or how they are structured. *[1 mark]*
[4 marks available in total]

d) A procedure taking a file name as a parameter. *[1 mark]*
Opening the file. *[1 mark]*
A condition-controlled loop to stop at the end of the file. *[1 mark]*
Using the toSpeech() procedure to read out each line. *[1 mark]*
Closing the file. *[1 mark]*
E.g.
procedure readAll(fileName)
  file = open(fileName)
  while NOT file.endOfFile()
    toSpeech(file.readLine())
  endwhile
  file.close()
endprocedure
It's important that you always remember to close a file once you're finished using it.

Section Seven — Design, Testing and IDEs

Page 78: Structured Programming

1 E.g.
- Indentation can improve readability by showing where different statements start and finish *[1 mark]* e.g. Jessica could indent within the IF / ELSE statement. *[1 mark]*
- Comments can be used to help explain the code *[1 mark]* e.g. on line 3 Jessica could include the comment // checks whether the base input is valid. *[1 mark]*
- Variable names can be used to make it easier to identify what the variables do *[1 mark]* e.g. Jessica could have given the variables 'num1' and 'num2' names like 'area' and 'base'. *[1 mark]*

2 a) E.g.

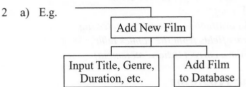

[3 marks available — 1 mark for correctly adding the module to the structure diagram, 1 mark for each suitable task within the module (up to 2 marks)]

b) Any **two** ways with valid explanations, e.g.
- Agreeing how and when to use comments will improve the maintainability *[1 mark]* as the team will be able to understand each other's code. *[1 mark]*
- Using clear indentation and spacing will improve the maintainability *[1 mark]* as it will be much easier to read and understand the code. *[1 mark]*
- Establishing and using naming conventions will improve the maintainability *[1 mark]* as the team will easily be able to understand what variables and sub programs are for. *[1 mark]*
- Agreeing how and when to use global variables will lead to fewer errors *[1 mark]* as each person's code is more likely to work with the other developers' code. *[1 mark]*
- Agreeing how to validate inputs will reduce errors *[1 mark]* as all parts of the program will accept similar inputs. *[1 mark]*
[4 marks available in total]

Page 79: Defensive Design

1 a) Checking data meets certain criteria before passing it into the program or database. *[1 mark]*

b) Any **two** suitable input validations, e.g.
- Check that the input value is an integer. *[1 mark]*
- Check that the input value is positive. *[1 mark]*
- Check that the input value is within the range of possible ages, e.g. less than 120. *[1 mark]*
[2 marks available in total]

c) Any **two** suitable input validations, e.g.
- Check that the string contains only letters and numbers. *[1 mark]*
- Check that the postcode is the correct length. *[1 mark]*
- Check that the postcode has the correct form, e.g. always ends with a number then two letters. *[1 mark]*
[2 marks available in total]

2 a) A means of confirming the identity of a user before they can access a program or part of a program. *[1 mark]*

b) E.g.
- The program deals with extremely sensitive personal data *[1 mark]* so it is important that information cannot be stolen or accessed by the wrong people. *[1 mark]*
- Different types of hospital staff may need to access the records *[1 mark]* so it will allow these different users access to the exact information they need and nothing more. *[1 mark]*
[2 marks available in total]

c) E.g. too much authentication can affect a program's functionality and put people off using it. *[1 mark]*

Pages 80-81: Testing

Warm-up

The statements that should be ticked are:
Using the wrong Boolean operator is a logic error.
Syntax errors will prevent code from running.

1 a) A type of error caused by the code not following the rules or grammar of the programming language. *[1 mark]*

   b) The code will translate and run *[1 mark]* but it will not behave as Huey intended. *[1 mark]*

2 a) Error: Missing bracket on line 3. *[1 mark]*
       Correction: print("Valid pincode") *[1 mark]*

   b) Error: Wrong Boolean operator in line 2. *[1 mark]*
       Correction: if pincode.length >= 4 AND pincode.length <= 6 then *[1 mark]*
       Tiffany's code currently allows any pincode length. Changing OR to AND makes sure only pincodes with lengths from 4 to 6 characters are allowed.

3 a) E.g. a test plan should take the user down all possible paths of the program. *[1 mark]* It should use normal, boundary (extreme), invalid and erroneous test data. *[1 mark]* If any of the tests get a result not equal to the expected outcome then the user knows there is a logic error. *[1 mark]*

   b)

Test Data	Expected Outcome	Reasons for test
groupSize = 4	210	Check program with data user is likely to input.
groupSize = 10	510	Check program works with values on the limit.
groupSize = 12	Display an error message	Check what happens if input is too large.

   [5 marks available — 1 mark per box]

4 a) i) The program is tested at the end of the development process. *[1 mark]* The whole program is tested at the same time to check that it's working correctly. *[1 mark]*

       ii) The program is tested while it is being developed. *[1 mark]* Different parts of the program (modules) are often tested separately. *[1 mark]*

   b) Any **one** advantage with explanation, e.g.
       • Only using final testing might make the development process quicker *[1 mark]* as he won't have to test each individual part of the program separately. *[1 mark]*

       Any **one** disadvantage with explanation, e.g.
       • Only using final testing might make it harder to locate an error, *[1 mark]* because the whole program is being tested at once. It will take longer to find and fix the error. *[1 mark]*
       [4 marks available in total]

Page 82: Trace Tables

1 a)

a	b
11	4
10	3
9	2
8	1
7	0

   [3 marks available — 1 mark for the correct first row, 1 mark for the correct second and third rows, 1 mark for the correct fourth and fifth rows]

   b) He should use *numDiff* *[1 mark]* because it returns the answer straight away regardless of the values of a and b. *diffNums* would have to repeat the WHILE loop many times if the values of a and b are both much greater than zero. *[1 mark]*
       Any sensible explanation will get you the second mark.

2 a)

k	arr[k]	x	y
		0	0
0	4	4	0
1	2		2
2	7	7	4
3	1		
4	9	9	7

   [4 marks available — 1 mark for each column with the correct values in the correct order]
   It doesn't matter if you've put spaces in different places to the table above, or if you've not got any spaces at all, as long as the values that each variable takes are correct.

   b) The algorithm finds the largest two numbers in an array of positive numbers *[1 mark]* and prints them, largest first. *[1 mark]*

Page 83: Translators

1 An interpreter *[1 mark]* translates the code as the program is running, one instruction at a time. *[1 mark]*
   A compiler *[1 mark]* translates all the source code in one go and creates an executable file. *[1 mark]*

2 a) Any **two** reasons, e.g.
       • They may need to have a greater control over the program in order to make a program with lower memory use. *[1 mark]*
       • They may need to have a greater control over what the CPU does in order to make a program run quicker. *[1 mark]*
       • They may be trying to maintain old code or hardware. *[1 mark]*
       [2 marks available in total]

   b) Assembly languages are more readable for humans than machine code *[1 mark]* so can be programmed / edited more easily. *[1 mark]*

3 Any **three** differences, e.g.
   • One instruction of high-level code represents many instructions of machine code, *[1 mark]* whereas one instruction of low-level code often represents one instruction of machine code. *[1 mark]*
   • High-level code works for many different machines and processors, *[1 mark]* whereas low-level languages normally only work for one type of machine or processor. *[1 mark]*
   • A programmer using a high-level language can easily store data without knowing about the memory structure, *[1 mark]* whereas a programmer using a low-level language needs to know how the CPU manages the memory. *[1 mark]*
   • Code written in a high-level language is easy for other programmers to understand and modify, *[1 mark]* whereas it is more difficult for other programmers to understand and modify code written in a low-level languages. *[1 mark]*
   [6 marks available in total]

Page 84: Integrated Development Environments

Warm-up

Code Editor: used for writing code.

Breakpoints: a debugging tool that stops the program at certain points.

Error Diagnostics: highlight errors in the program.

1 a) A translator turns the source code into machine code *[1 mark]* allowing Cynthia to run the application. *[1 mark]*
       Error Diagnostics highlight errors in the code *[1 mark]* allowing Cynthia to easily find and fix errors in her application. *[1 mark]*
       A Code editor allows the user to enter code and includes features like indenting, auto-correct, line numbering and colour coding *[1 mark]* making it a lot easier for Cynthia to write and maintain her application. *[1 mark]*

b) The translator will pick up syntax errors as it will be unable to translate the code. *[1 mark]* These errors along with their location will be shown in the error diagnostics panel. *[1 mark]* The code editor lets Cynthia navigate to the correct line and correct the error. *[1 mark]*

2 E.g.
- Run-time environment runs the program within the IDE *[1 mark]* so Max can see which part of the code is running when the logic errors occur. *[1 mark]*
- Breakpoints allow Max to stop the program on certain lines as the program is running *[1 mark]* allowing Max to gather information about the values of particular variables. *[1 mark]*
- Error diagnostics will alert Max to possible errors, e.g. using the wrong data type *[1 mark]* which may be causing logic errors even though it is not breaking the language syntax. *[1 mark]*

[4 marks available in total]

Pages 85-86: Mixed Questions

1 a) Erroneous test data has an incorrect data type and should not be accepted by the program. *[1 mark]* Using them in testing will make sure that the user can enter any data without breaking the program. *[1 mark]*

b) i) Type of data: Normal *[1 mark]*
Intended Outcome: 20 *[1 mark]*
Actual Outcome: 20 *[1 mark]*

ii) Type of data: Invalid *[1 mark]*
Intended Outcome: User receives an error message, e.g. "Invalid dice score, please re-enter." *[1 mark]*
Actual Outcome: 19 *[1 mark]*
The game uses a six-sided dice, so if the user inputs a 9 they should receive an error message. However, Tony's program does not check for this, so it will still run if invalid data is entered.

c) Any **two** ways, e.g.
- He could make sure only integers are accepted. *[1 mark]*
- He could make sure only the numbers from 1 to 6 are accepted. *[1 mark]*
- He could ensure that the input is only one character long. *[1 mark]*
- He could make sure that only Yes/No, yes/no, Y/N, y/n, etc. are accepted for the "Roll again" prompt. *[1 mark]*

[2 marks available in total]

2 a) Logic error: for x = 0 to 10 *[1 mark]*
Explanation: The email address may be longer than eleven characters. *[1 mark]*

b) Comments *[1 mark]* would explain aspects of the code so they are understood by other developers. *[1 mark]*
This is the only possible answer because Natasha's code uses indentation and clearly named variables already.

c) Any **one** way with an explanation, e.g.
- Most email addresses end in a similar way. *[1 mark]* Use a whitelist to check that the ending is valid, for example, .co.uk or .com. *[1 mark]*
- Check the email address contains a '.' character *[1 mark]* as most email addresses will contain a full stop. *[1 mark]*

[2 marks available in total]

d) Any **two** ways, e.g.
- A compiler would produce an executable file *[1 mark]* while an interpreter would not. *[1 mark]*
- A compiler would list any errors at the end of the translation *[1 mark]* while an interpreter would return the first error it found then stop. *[1 mark]*
- A compiler would translate the code all at once *[1 mark]* while an interpreter would translate and run the code line by line. *[1 mark]*

[4 marks available in total]

3 E.g.
- The code editor might include an auto-indentation feature *[1 mark]* which will make the code clearer to read. *[1 mark]*
- The code editor might include an auto-colour feature *[1 mark]* which makes it easier to distinguish between different features of the code, e.g. variables and comments. *[1 mark]*
- Finding logic errors requires a lot of work by the user — the IDE has debugging tools to help *[1 mark]* but most of the work is done through testing. *[1 mark]*
- The IDE won't be able to tell if clear variable names and comments have been used *[1 mark]* so it won't be able to help with this, it's up to the developer. *[1 mark]*
- The IDE can't check if programmers have used a consistent approach in different parts of the program *[1 mark]* so it will be up to the developers to maintain good practice. *[1 mark]*

[6 marks available in total]